This book is for

_____

This book comes to you
With a drop of my love,
To caress you
And comfort you,
And hold your hand,
And lead you to take tiny steps.
At each step, gently unfurling
Until you begin to remember
The wonderful person
I know you are.

From Mikyla
xx

How to Love and Be Loved ♡

by Mikyla Limpkin

Contents

PAUSE
& REFLECT

preface   start here

preliminaries

introduction
          °°

beginning   prologue

preamble

Introduction

PAUSE
& REFLECT

Just For You

Just For You

I wrote this book because I'm a romantic. I want everyone to love and be loved. What's more I actually believe it's possible. Actually I don't just believe, I know. There are many things that we are taught in our lives but how to love and be loved isn't one of them.

I want there to be less pain and more love in the world. I want to create joy and make celebrations. I want to create joy in your life. I want you to join me in the revolution of love. Like I said, I'm a romantic.

If you have a sneaky suspicion that life could be better, then this book is aimed at you. If you're struggling and want something better, then this book is aimed at you. If you feel a lack of love, then this book is aimed at you.

I want everyone
to love and be loved.

If you're stuck on a sofa, overwhelmed and with no obvious way off, then this book is for you. Whether you've had highly paid jobs or lowly paid jobs or no-pay jobs, this book is for you. That sofa glue is a good leveller. Insufficient love is not dependent on your level of education or wage, not on your job nor your status. If you want to feel more love, more life, this book is for you.

I started writing this book before Covid struck. It's a culmination of years of personal and professional experience, observations, research and training, workshops and community groups. I trained thirty years ago as a product designer in a traditional, industrial British institution but also in a very vibrant, creative French one. I was taught to research, conceptualise, develop and test designs. I've spent my life designing projects rather than products. Always aiming to improve people's lives. Sometimes I was highly paid, sometimes I was lowly paid, sometimes I wasn't paid at all but I have always been doing the same thing: Observing, thinking, researching, bringing together ideas, bringing together people, always trying to create a positive impact.

I've worked all around England from inner cities to remote rural areas listening to people's needs and working with them to design and deliver solutions. I've met diverse people in diverse areas. I learnt so much from them about their communities and the issues they all faced, but they all wanted the same thing; for their lives, and the lives of those around them to be better.

Some people still stand out, even though I've forgotten their names:

The seamstress, who when asked by the kids on her estate where she got her embroidered jeans, invited them into her home and taught them how to embroider on their own jeans.

The environmentalist who noticed how much good wood was being wasted in the building trade and set up a wood recycling scheme which by demonstrating the value of the waste, changed the habits of the builders.

The woman who cracked the issue of working and childcare years before child daycare existed by opening a corner shop with two friends taking turns to mind their collective children in the room above the shop.

The man who set up a mechanics workshop teaching teenagers how to fix engines of go-karts and keep on the straight and narrow.

Everyone of these people taught me and inspired me. Unfortunately along the way I experienced some of the really bad things that can happen to a person that knock them down. Unbelievable things in fact. So painful that I longed to die before I awoke. But I didn't die. I still existed. But I didn't live.

So in disgust, I turned my back on the manmade world. I dropped out, grew veg, grew babies. I cooked, I sewed, I picked apples, I made jam.

I looked up. I looked down. I looked around. My design skills kicked in. I found a way out. I read, I observed, I experimented, I learnt, I designed, I tested, I designed again. I discovered strategies to love and be loved.

I used these strategies daily and from then on, whenever I stumbled into a hole it was never as deep as the last one and I was never down it as long. My holes became shallower and less frequent. I learnt how to avoid them.

I discovered
strategies to love and be loved.

I realised that if I wrote down my knowledge, in an accessible way, it could be shared more widely, then I could help other people climb out of holes. I could help others to love and be loved.

Then Covid struck and during the first lockdown I found that I became my own audience. I had to work hard to keep my family well. I alone had to keep my little ship afloat. My book became my mentor. It wasn't meant for me, it was meant for you, but Covid put us all back in the same boat.

I realised that what I'd been writing was a manual for how to write a Life Manual. A manual personalised just for you, full of tips and strategies that you can test and find what works for you. Techniques and habits to keep you well, keep you going, help you follow your dreams. A manual that once written you can refer to whenever you need some help to get back on track.

A manual for how to write a Life Manual, a manual personalised just for you.

When Covid sent me some new holes to fall into I found my friends giving me back advice I'd given to them. I found I needed it and it worked. This convinced me that I really had to get this knowledge out there. I'd read so much and learnt so much but the big issue was how to make this information accessible. I wanted the information to get to the people who need it, the people who could make practical use of it, who aren't interested in studying the theory of it. And I'm trained as a designer.

I remembered that when I was a kid, we had cars that needed regular maintenance to keep working but even so they often broke down. Dads had the job of mending them or roping in some other dads to get the job done. Or at least that's how it seemed in my home as my dad was an engineer and into his cars.

We had cool cars; a Volkswagen Beetle like Herbie, a bubble car, a Bond, a Reliant Robin just like Delboy (apparently that one was so my mum could drive it with just a motorbike driving licence).

They all seemed to come with Haynes Manuals which had wonderful illustrations of car engines and detailed instructions of how to take engines apart and how to put them back together. I learnt that everything was fixable, it was just dependent on how much effort you were willing to make.

Everything that ever went wrong on our cars or needed maintenance could be identified by a page marked with oily fingerprints. Even now the smell of Swafega hand cleaner is pervading my senses as I write. Every type of car had its own manual. We had one for our VW Beetle, another for our Ford Capri (nauseating to travel in the back of that one), one for our Vauxhall Viva (bare legs stick to the seats in the hot weather in that one). Every manual was specific to a range of years. If your Ford Fiesta was a 1980 model it was a different manual to the 1985 manual.

Every car was different, even the ones that you'd think were the same. And so it is with people. We might look the same but we're all different. We come apart and are put back together slightly differently to the next model. We all need regular maintenance and sometimes have breakdowns or bits drop off. Regular servicing is a good idea.

We all need regular maintenance and sometimes have breakdowns or bits drop off. Regular servicing is a good idea.

So this is what my book is. It's a manual for you, just for you. It's yours to mark up with oily thumb prints and highlighter pens. It's value will be decreed by the scribbles in the margins, the turned down corners, the sticky notes hanging out and the crinkled bit from where it got damp being read in the bath.

As you read through this book, you can experiment with all different types of maintenance and fixes. You'll figure out or recognise what works for you. Then I'll show you how to collect together all the best bits for you and make a little reference book, a real thing you can hold in your hand, unique for you that you can keep and refer to whenever you need to maintain or service or fix a bit that's about to fall off. A little book made of paper and cardboard, sewn together with four clever bookbinding stitches. I'll show you mine and I'd so love it if you'd show me yours.

Oh and a note about **Indigo Violet**. She arrived on the scene. Quite unexpectedly. She climbed out one day, from a box of drawing inks I'd been given for my birthday.

She was quite a distraction but she made me very happy and my friends seemed to like her and apparently their friends did too.

Not content with the confines of a sketch pad Indigo Violet took herself off to the beach and then put selfies on Instagram. She even managed to waltz into an artist's magazine and began discussing a modelling job. Then having got a taste for a modicum of fame, she started poking through my writing and inserting her nose here there and was often able to explain my point better than I could, sometimes demanding I draw a little doodle.

Eventually to placate her I gave her own page on my website **thecompanyofsmiles.co.uk/art** and I know she'll find a way into the print copy of this book.

Visit www.thecompanyofsmiles.co.uk/art

PAUSE
& REFLECT

Bigger Than The
Two Of Us

Bigger Than The Two Of Us

I have learnt that when some of us are left to our own devices, we tend to dwell on the bad stuff that happened.

When we view the world through those experiences it's as if we are wearing grey tinted glasses. If we could find some rose tinted specs to wear the world would look different wouldn't it?

You'll notice that the world treats rose-spec wearers differently to what we may be used to. We just need to find those specs.

I've met many people who are struggling in life. Surviving not living. I'm sure there are many more since Covid struck. The Pandemic stopped us in our tracks but when we are stopped, when starting up again is slow and requires focussed effort, we have the time to peruse the choices, the freedom to choose our focus. There is another way, other than this daily grind. We just have to start by wanting it. Positive changes can happen so fast in ways you never expect nor could ever predict. We just need faith. Faith in love.

With a teeny tiny bit of faith in love we can make teeny tiny changes that, without any extra effort from us, will grow into something far far bigger. Together we can change the world!

Positive changes can happen so fast in ways you never expect nor could ever predict.

How tiny is a tomato seed? We've all eaten these gelatinous seeds as juicy fresh tomatoes. When the seeds are dried for saving, they shrink to teeny tiny. Save one on a piece of tissue paper and watch and see it shrink.

Have you ever sown one of these teeny tiny seeds on your window sill? Did you lovingly transplant the little plants into bigger and bigger pots and put them outside your door, carefully watering and feeding them, protecting them from harsh weather? Did they produce delicious ripe tomatoes for you to pick and eat? Until the weather cooled and they ripened no more, and the plant went yellow, and dry, and died and was no more?

To sow those teeny tiny seeds you had to have faith that your tiny effort would enable the creation of something new, something bigger, something greater than the seed in your hand. Just a tiny bit of faith was all you needed.

With that tiny bit of faith, you took a tiny little action, that tiny little action created a far bigger change in your life than you could achieve alone. There was something more than just you.

Have you ever eaten a pear and held the pear pip in the palm of your hand and just looked at it? Looked at its seamless smoothness and pointy tip? Have you ever wondered at how from such tininess can spring a whole tree? A tree as tall as fifteen meters high like the mighty Perry Pear, full of hundreds and hundreds of pears?

How every year, hundreds and hundreds of pears can grow on a tree, that once was a pip?

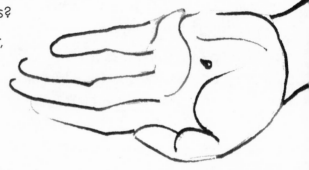

The tree grows itself without you lifting a finger except to harvest a juicy fruit, to grasp a ripe pear between finger and thumb and to twist and release it from the tree.

So how big do you think a tiny amount of love could grow? How much would it multiply, all by itself, without you lifting a finger, once released from your care? Why not try and find out?

If we wanted a pear seed to grow, we'd have to consciously put it in the optimal conditions, choosing a place with the right amount of heat, light and water, then nature would do the rest. From the seed would grow a tree. It's not like we have to build the tree with hammer and nails or sculpt a branch with hammer and chisel. The pear seed would do its own thing. We just have to help start it off.

What if we did the same thing with a seed of love? What if we gave it the right conditions to grow, what would it grow into? What would it become? Together we can choose love. The revolution has already started and if you're reading this book, it looks like you're wanting to join.

So how big do you think a tiny amount of love could grow?

So come on, choose this path with me. Let me hold your hand and together take one tiny step, make one tiny change, see what happens.

Let me tell you a story about the big bad wolf. Once upon a time, in about the year 1920, the last pack of wolves roaming the 3,472 square miles of the Yellowstone National Park in the USA, were killed. Dead all dead.

With no wolves left to eat them, the deer population of elk flourished. As the elk population increased they ate more and more vegetation and devastated the habitats of other wildlife. In particular the abundance of elks' munching leaves severely damaged the areas of willow trees at the river edges which meant there weren't enough trees for beavers to thrive there. So beaver numbers dwindled to just one colony. That huge huge park and only one beaver colony.

This is the kind of thing that scientists around the world study. When the top predator in the food chain, in this case the wolf, is removed, dramatic changes are caused to the ecosystem.

However this story takes an unusual twist.

In 1995 a pack of 8 wolves was reintroduced to Yellowstone and what happened next surprised the scientists. The wolves predictably munched through some of the elk population, but in their deaths, the elks benefited others. The carcasses of these wolf kills provided food for scavenger creatures like grizzly bears, eagles and ravens. So grizzly bears, eagles and ravens began to thrive.

Meanwhile, because they had a new hunter, the big bad wolf, the elk population became more timid, keeping more to the safety of the trees and so didn't munch the willow trees at the river edges. The willow trees were therefore greener and healthier and so supported more wildlife.

In particular the willow trees helped the beavers to thrive. Because the deer stopped destroying the river willow, the trees grew tall. Large enough for the beavers to fell and use the wood to build more dams.

Beavers need dams to make 'lodges' where they can safely rear their young without their babies becoming someone's breakfast. More dams meant more beavers were reared. More beavers meant more dams were built. More dams meant that the river was slowed and new lakes were created. The slower, shadier river created more shaded water that fish like so there were more fish too. The new lakes meant that water was stored up for drier times so where habitats had previously dried out in the sun and disappeared, these habitats instead survived the hot weather and contributed to the diversity of wildlife and vegetation.

Then along came a wonderful word, 'cascade'. Are you imagining wonderful waterfalls? Or a solar fountain outside your door with a series of ceramic pots playing a water melody? Well there's another. **The cascade effect.**

A Yellowstone wildlife biologist is quoted as saying,

> *"the presence of wolves triggered a still unfolding cascade effect among animals and plants, one that will take decades of research to understand."*

(www.yellowstonepark.com)

The cascade he's talking about here is the food chain. Bear with me here, there is a point to be made.

Now, the food chain is the major system of the natural world. Little things are eaten by bigger things which in turn are eaten by even bigger things and so it goes on. Mankind likes to position himself at the top but in Yelllowstone Park,

it's the wolves who are at the top of the food chain because nothing eats them.

Now adding or taking away the species at the top of the foodchain has a special name in biological terms. It's called a 'Trophic Cascade'.

Back to us humans and our society.

I believe that 'human motivation' is the major system of our human world. I believe that if we reintroduce love to the top of our human world, we can begin something like a Trophic Cascade that will bring dramatic changes into the structure of the world as we know it; A Love Cascade. If we all, as individuals, introduce love at the top of our own lives and our own little ecosystems, then the cascade effect will astound us.

If we all, as individuals introduce love at the top of our own lives and our own little ecosystems then the cascade effect will astound us.

"In the entire scientific literature, there are only five or six comparable circumstances [to Yellowstone Park's Trophic Cascade]. What we're seeing now is a feeding frenzy of scientific research."

- Doug Smith, Biologist, Yellowstone Park

What this biologist is telling us is that cases of Trophic Cascades, where something is added instead of taken away, are so rare that they haven't been studied much.

To me, this indicates that in our modern world, where we're always being told that 'we are led by the science', scientists actually cannot predict what amazing things can or will happen, when we drop something positive into the top of our system. As Doug Smith says, there simply haven't been enough examples to study.

If wolves can change rivers, what could a tiny drop of your love do?

When the managers at Yellowstone Park chose to work with the natural world, rather than fighting against it, (as some 'conservation work' tries to do) then amazing, unpredicted things happened. The wolves literally changed the course of the river. The world of the park started healing itself.

So if wolves can change rivers, what could a tiny grain of your love do? Could it heal the world?

So that's it really.
I'm talking about a Cascade of Love.
It all starts with just one tiny drop of love.

Here is mine to you...

PAUSE
& REFLECT

How to use this book

How to use this book

This book is Part One of a series. I designed it that way to pace the information and avoid overwhelming you. It's the beginning of the journey which will continue in Part Two.

Sign up to The Company of Smiles:

www.thecompanyofsmiles.co.uk to be the first to know when subsequent parts are released.

I've written Part One so that you can read it cover to cover, but also that you can dip in and dip out of it, taking what you need when you need to.

As I said, I'm a great believer in book graffiti. I'd like nothing better than for you to fold down the corner of pages (admittedly tricky with an ebook), highlight pertinent paragraphs, add your own thoughts in the margin and generally make my book your own.

Don't think of keeping this book pristine to lend out to friends, it's yours! Scribble all over it and let them get their own copy. This one's for you. Just you. And I want you to rebel against everything your teachers ever told you about looking after books. The more dogeared or highlighted the better. The more personalised the better.

I'll even give you my blessing to add to my drawings. Indigo Violet could do with some clothes before she catches a chill. She's not the most modest of people but you could take control of that. Draw on some new outfits and see what she thinks.

At the end of each chapter is the start of your personalised manual. There's a page called Takeaways. This is where I want you to pause and reflect on the last chapter and write down notes of what resonates with you, what works for you and anything else that you want to remember that you read or that popped into your head. Write down as much as you can because then when we get to the last chapter you'll have all the content you need to make your own Life Manual.

If you're reading this paperback, write it on paper, if it's an e-book use a dedicated notebook. The trick to writing your own manual is to be able to recognise what works for you and to jot it down in a way you can easily find it again.

I like to use little symbols alongside notes because these can quickly be recognised as you skim through. A bit like how £ and $ symbols make it easy to spot money in a list of numbers. So as you're writing down your notes, if a symbol that has meaning for you pops into your head, scribble it down. It's all about effective communication for you, not gallery hangable artwork.

It's critical to be able to write when you want to and hunting down a pen often loses the moment. If like me you find yourself plagued by pen Borrowers, try tying one end of a piece of ribbon to your pen and looping the other end around the book spine and central page (of this book or your notebook), like a ribbon book mark that lies in a book. I find that rather generously, there are lengths of gift ribbon sewn into the shoulders of ladies' tops to help with transporting garments on hangers. Cut these out, tie several together if necessary to make the right length, knot the ribbon to itself to secure it and hey presto! The Borrowers are thwarted! Or perhaps they don't live in your house, just mine.

A Ships Log

A ship's log charts the sea conditions, weather and progress of a voyage. I've made a Ship's Log for you to use to chart the progress of your journey. This will help you begin to notice your internal weather, the external conditions and your headway. Keep your Ship's Log somewhere where you'll see it whether that's as a bookmark in your notebook or stuck to your fridge door.

Download the Ship's Log from **www.thecompanyofsmiles.co.uk/to-love-and-be-loved**.

I wish you fair passage, calm sunny waters

and a gentle breeze driving you forwards...

PAUSE
& REFLECT

Shopping List

Shopping List

In addition to a copy of this book, you will need a lined notebook and a pen to keep alongside it. Make sure your notebook is beautiful to you. Choose a notebook that you like the cover of or...

Have a play... Decorate a cheap notebook with a postcard, a photo, a beautiful piece of coloured paper or wrapping paper, a picture cut from a magazine or even your own doodles. Anything that makes you feel good. If you want to make it more durable you can cover it with sticky-back plastic, lots of strips of sellotape (if you don't mind the lines) or you can paint it with white PVA craft glue that acts like a varnish.

If you're serious about bringing about changes then you need to 'do the work' as they say.

Reading a book will create some change but the big stuff happens when you actually apply yourself a tiny bit everyday and take tiny step after tiny step. None of us like a chore but all of us like a pleasure, so make sure your note book is a pleasure, that it is as beautiful to you as it can possibly be, a joy to pick up (I once bought a harsh hairy one by mistake - ugh!), a thing of beauty to admire each day and will be something you want to interact with.

I am a bit of a notebook nut and have found that the more my notebook/journal is stunningly beautiful, the more I want to write in it and the more it feels like a supportive friend to me.

If you hated school, avoid anything that reminds you of your school books, whether that's colour or size or thickness. As I said, the more positive you feel about your notebook the better.

As a notebook nut, I have fallen into the trap of not using a bought notebook because it's so beautiful. I 'keep it for best' and never use it. This is immensely silly of me because I get so much more pleasure from handling a beautiful notebook every day than I do a utilitarian one. Your notebook is the beginning of being kind to yourself - choose a beautiful notebook and use it!

A Kindly Book

Your note book will actually be your very kind friend. The kindly person we'd all love to have in our lives. Perhaps we should call it our Kindly Book? It loves you and cherishes you and likes nothing better than hearing of your news. As you progress through my books, I'll also tell you about the Candy Floss Pages which will require your beautiful note book. Your Kindly Book.

Every time something good happens in your head or in your life you can write it down in your book with the date. You can share your successes with this lovely, kind, caring friend (your Kindly Book) who wants to celebrate all things good, particularly your successes. This friend (your Kindly book) will eventually become a source of support and comfort, telling you all the good stuff about you, all the good things in your life that are starting to happen and how to make more happen.

Introduction Takeaways

Use the Takeaways page at the end of each chapter to note down any points that you want to remember that resonate with you or that you need to remember to do. Your notes here will be the basis of your very own life manual.

Make your mark on this page now!

Yes, I am shouting, but in a kind and teasing kind of way and with a big grin on my face because I really want you to make your mark on this book. No more clean pristine pages, I want you to claim them as yours!

Not with your bestest handwriting and with your bestest pen, any old quill or charred stick will do, or pen, or pencil. The first challenge is to just conquer the fear of the blank page. It only takes a millisecond, then it's done.

If you've nothing to write, worry not. Draw an emoji. Any one will do. Once it's done, this book is truly yours and you're truly on your way. Congratulations.

Congratulate yourself.

I am. I'm here cheering you on.

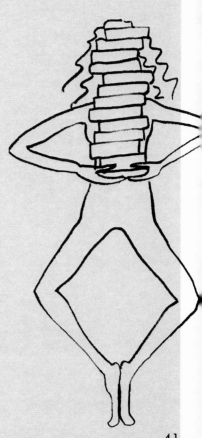

PAUSE
& REFLECT

*Chapter One
Getting Started*

PAUSE
& REFLECT

Gratitude

Gratitude

I thought long and hard about what should be the first thing to do. A practical exercise is the easiest thing to do. If I said start by putting your thumb on your nose, you could do it. You picked up this book, so you could touch your nose with your thumb. Go on. Prove my point. I've just done it. Now your turn. Easy wasn't it? However if I started by saying change a habit, that would be harder wouldn't it?

I seem to have developed a habit of munching when I'm cold, and it's been cold a lot lately and I have grown a corresponding layer of insulation. Stopping munching when I'm cold is hard. I know that because having observed a marshmallow body in my bathtub, I decided to stop munching. Unfortunately it's still cold and I'm still nurturing my personal insulation. So, to conclude, changing habits is hard.

Even harder are our belief systems. How many years has it taken for the belief in global warming to become mainstream?

Beliefs are hard and slow to change and tend to need lots of evidence. However I'm going start with beliefs. This is day one and I'm going to start with your beliefs.

The world looks a pretty depressing place at the moment, full of Covid. Our lives have changed beyond belief. But, I challenge you to find one thing to be thankful

Changing habits is hard.
Even harder are our belief systems.

for because the biggest transformations come from re-learning to be thankful. It is such a simple sounding thing but the results are more profound than you would ever believe - until you try it.

Let's do an exercise together:

Get a glass out of your kitchen. Fill it to the half way mark with a drink of your choice, let's say it's orange juice. Now look at it. Is it half full or half empty? What do you normally see? A glass half full or a glass half empty? Write down your answer.

Maybe you saw a half empty glass and thought what a shame it is that you only have half a glass of orange to drink. Let's flip that and say instead 'aren't I lucky to have some juice!'

You see the glass is always half full and half empty at the same time. That bit doesn't change. However it's your choice which way you want to view it. Everyone has this choice. It's an incredibly simple, but incredibly powerful choice to make. You can choose to see the bit you want in your life and focus on that, or you could keep seeing the void, the empty bit, the lack of what you want in your life.

Look at your glass again and take it further: 'All that orange juice, all ready prepared in the glass. Someone else has squeezed the juice from the orange for me. Someone else picked it from the tree for me. Yet someone else watered and tended the tree all year to produce the best crop of fruit, just so that I could have this orange juice in a glass to drink'.

Nothing needs to change for you to practise being thankful. You just have to look for the good bits and notice them and be prepared to flip the bad bits so you can see the good bits. Being thankful directs your life on an upward spiral. It surely can't be that simple can it? Maybe you think you have to have a wonderful charmed life to start with in order to do this? You don't. From the lowest starting points you can choose thankfulness over despair or bitterness and life will get better.

I was listening to the Ted Talk 'Why ambitious women have flat heads' by Dame Stephanie Shirley who became an incredibly successful tech entrepreneur back in the 1960's before we'd really heard of tech let alone high flying businesswomen (which is why incidentally she called herself 'Steve' initially). Dame Stephanie's success is remarkable by any standards and it would seem that it isn't limited to her career because she talks about a very supportive and happy marriage too. What struck me

Nothing needs to change for you to practise being thankful. You just have to look for the good bits and notice them.

though in her Ted Talk was her lifelong expression of deep gratitude.

"All that I am, stems from when I got onto a train in Vienna [in 1939], part of the Kinder Transport which saved 10,000 children from Nazi Europe. I was five years old." She was vibrant and vital and eighty-two when she gave this talk. "I am only alive because so long ago I was helped by generous strangers. I was lucky" - www. ted.com (2015).

From a standing start, this refugee accumulated wealth in excess of £150 million. Her thankfulness not only sent her life in a upward spiral, but it made her act in exceptionally kind ways too. She made seventy of her employees instant millionaires when she gave them shares and then floated her business. Then she turned philanthropist making donations of untold millions. Her gratitude continues: "I love England with a passion as perhaps only someone who's lost their human rights can feel. I decided to make mine a life that was worth saving".

Thanks to the Kinder Transport, Dame Stephanie Shirley wasn't one of the six million Jews killed by the Nazis. Clearly her life could so easily have been shaped by bitterness and hatred but like other survivors I've heard interviewed, she chose an alternative path. One of positivity.

I wrote to Dame Stephanie Shirley with my observations on her attitude of gratitude, asking for her comments. Her reply to me was: "My survivor guilt led to ongoing depression which only lifted properly when I started to devote my life to philanthropy. Today I am a genuinely happy person."

So my conclusion is that her thankfulness for the kindness she received from the Kinder Transport enabled her to drive her life forward with a positive force but it was her paying forward this kindness that healed her wounds (I'll talk more about kindness later).

Steve Shirley's story is famous because it involves huge financial wealth and huge financial philanthropy which is easy to measure and makes the headlines. However there are many other hugely successful, hugely thankful people whose successes are far harder to measure because no money is involved, just the transforming power of love, like some of the youth work social entrepreneurs I mentioned. This kind of success rarely makes one famous but it's success just the same.

So next time you hear an incredible, successful, passionate person being interviewed, listen out for signs that they practise gratitude. It's not simply that their success has made them thankful. I believe it's the other way round, that for them it is the consciously being thankful that has enabled their success. Once you start actively being thankful, more and more good

Next time you hear an incredible, successful, passionate person being interviewed, listen out for signs that they practise gratitude.

things start coming your way. Practising gratitude is a very safe exercise to try because there is nobody sitting in judgment on your achievements. Nobody has to know you're doing it. Nobody will be trying to measure your results. This is a very private action and only you will know you're doing it. Gratitude is a matter of perspective.

When I was living in a concrete city and missing my village life and country walks it was easy for me to feel homesick for the abundance of the natural world in the countryside. Wherever I looked there were grey buildings and grey roads and grey pavements.

So much grey and decay. Once neat lines of paving slabs had been shattered by errant heavy lorries mounting them. In the cracks urban detritus had gathered and weeds had started to germinate like tufts of body hair. Then one day, into my mind popped the lyrics to a joyous song, "I saw the grass growing through the cracks of the pavement" a victorious song about the triumph of nature and I smiled a big smile and my mood was lifted. Suddenly I saw hope and optimism and the power of nature springing from the broken slabs.

Being thankful is about viewing the same world but noticing the good bits, not the bad. Seeing hope, not despair. Having had such a horrific start to life, Dame Stephanie Shirley had a head start on gratitude. Most of us don't have such an extreme starting place, but look where it got her.

Now that I've made you grateful for your half empty glass, we're going to keep practising gratitude. A good tip is that you only have to be grateful for what you have now, this minute. The past is gone, the future is yet to come but now is now. If you are focussing on now, today, this minute even, what have you got to be thankful for?

Think of one thing that you are grateful for.

We're going to try to do this everyday and do this as soon as we wake up. It may be hard at first, but it's really, really powerful.

If you're struggling to find something to be grateful for, look in the gaps, just like the gaps in the pavement: What's there? I always remember the advice that if your child is screaming in a tantrum and can't seem to be calmed down (and you're about to join in the screaming yourself) look for the gaps. At some point the child will have to draw breath and at the moment you say 'Oh well done for calming yourself down!'. Obviously you have to say this incredibly quickly because those gaps don't last long, but you repeat repeat repeat and it does work.

So let's get going. If you're in a e-book, you'll need to have your Kindly Book to hand as well as your Ship's Log (which you can print out, fold in half and use as a

Being thankful is about viewing the same world, but noticing the good bits, not the bad.

bookmark in your Kindly Book). If you have an IRL book (in-real-life book) aka a paperback, then you have the choice of book graffiti or writing in your Kindly Book but you too will also need to print your Ship's Log.

Print out your Ship's Log from

www.thecompanyofsmiles.co.uk.

You only have
to be grateful for what
you have now, this minute.

The past is gone,
the future is yet to come
but now is now.

Practising Gratitude

Let's get scribbling in this book, to practise here what you'll eventually do in your Kindly Book.

Across the page, we're going to **write** today's date and **colour** in the heart. Below this we're going to write down one thing for today that we're thankful for. When you start doing this in your Kindly Book, as you fill up the pages, you can flick back and see all the hearts and know how full of wonderful things your life is. We're going to work up to writing three things each day, but one will do for today unless that is, you're bubbling over with gratitude. If you are, jump straight in with three thankfuls. One heart for each.

Here's mine:

"Today I am thankful for the peace and tranquility around me that enables me to get on with writing my book."

What I haven't said is that one of my children keeps interrupting me. I'm choosing to focus instead on the fact that I am actually managing to get some writing done. I could however add another thankful that "I am grateful for all the pink coloured joy that having a little girl in my life brings".

That's because she's been contacting me on video call and fills most of the screen with a lovely shade of pink pyjamas. A shade that I find especially beautiful, suits her so well and is so archetypal of 'little girl' which I know she won't stay as for long. I choose not to focus on the fact

that she keeps interrupting me when she knows I'm trying
to work and that she still hasn't got washed and dressed...

Day 1: date here **Today I am thankful for...**

Let's keep track of your progress to inspire you that
life is changing for the better: **Colour** in a heart in
your Ship's Log and add the date.

You may want to pause reading this book here and
just focus over the next week on this gratitude exercise,
before you read the next bit of the book.

Day 2

Write one thankful and **colour** in a heart on your Ship's Log. Is today, yesterday's tomorrow? Did you remember a thankful the day following when you started? Don't worry if you didn't, try for two in a row starting now.

Day 1: date here

Today I am thankful for...

Day 3

Write two thankfuls and **colour** in a heart on your Ship's Log. If you forget and miss a day, don't worry, just keep going! Better luck remembering tomorrow.

Day 1: date here

Today I am thankful for...

and...

Day 4

Write two thankfuls and **colour** in a heart on your Ship's Log. Is it getting easier to remember yet?

Day 1: date here

Today I am thankful for...

and...

58

Write two thankfuls and **colour** in a heart on your Ship's Log. I think you're getting the idea now.

Day 1: date here   Today I am thankful for...

and...

Day 6

Write three thankfuls and **colour** in a heart on your Ship's Log. Wow you're really taking to this!

Day 1: date here

Today I am thankful for...

and...

and...

Day 7

Write three thankfuls and **colour** in a heart on your Ship's Log. Seven days! Well done!

Day 7: date here **Today I am thankful for...**

and...

and...

61

When a whole week has gone by (or you've filled in seven days of thankfuls if you're a bit hit and miss still with the daily habit) you'll have been thankful at least 12 times.

This is the beginning of a habit.

The world is becoming a brighter place.

This is evidence for you to believe that life is good.

Use your Kindly Book from now on, aiming to write three thankfuls every morning, as soon after you wake up as possible, to set your day off on a positive note. Don't forget to put a heart in the margin so you can see at a glance that good things are happening in your life!

Start noticing the hearts.

You will.

They're there.

It just takes a little practice to be able to see them. Bit like foraging for mushrooms - they're well camouflaged at first until you get your eye in.

PAUSE
& REFLECT

A New Brain

A New Brain

Ever wished you could take your head off and swap it for another? One that works more in your favour? Well I'm here to tell you you can! No surgery even required!

Sometimes our brain can work in ways that are not beneficial to us and these suboptimal ways of working show up as mental health problems or mental illness. Psychiatrists used to think that only medication could change the way our brains operate. However, now thanks to modern brain scanning technology, it has been shown that changes in our thinking and feeling can create changes in how our brains work.

Don't you think it's amazing that changes in our thinking and feelings are visible (given the right viewing equipment)? What happens is our thoughts and our feelings can actually increase or decrease the blood flow in specific areas of our brain.

Our thoughts and our feelings can change the electrical activity in parts of our brain. These changes are known as brain plasticity, or neuro-plasticity. It's the biological, chemical and physical ability for the brain to change itself. It's proven.

So we can change our brains with our thoughts! Amazing! Isn't that good news? If you want a new brain, you can think one into existence! You can feel one into existence!

Let's give it a go.

We can change our brains with our thoughts!

Getting Started Takeaways

Write down things that struck a chord / things you want to remember or use for your Life Manual.

PAUSE
& REFLECT

Chapter Two
Get Into Your Body

PAUSE
& REFLECT

Standing Up For Yourself

Standing Up For Yourself

We are all lucky enough to have human bodies. Imagine if you were suddenly cast into the body of a jelly fish, and could only float in the sea, bobbing along with the current and waves? Our human bodies are amazing. Let me tell you, you have a great body. You really do. Your body is amazing, and now that I've told you what a great body you have, it's time to stand up for yourself.

I often find myself standing up, in queues. I am English after all. When I commuted on public transport there was a lot of standing around, waiting for transport that was over-crowded, late, noisy, smelly. Not a lot to be said for it really. People always comment that Londoners are such a miserable lot, and as I spent an hour every morning travelling 10 miles across London to work, much of it spent in a noisy, hot, smelly hole in the ground, I always thought misery was an understandable response. However in one yoga session, we were challenged to stand tall, as if we had a puppet string coming out the top of our head and pulling our bodies upwards.

We had to rock back and forth on our bare feet, spreading the weight from our heels to our toes, until our weight was equally spread between the two. We had to spread our toes wide to enable greater balance. We had to rotate our shoulders one at a time, forward, up, back and down to make sure they were in the correct position.

If they were, we'd find our hands dangled loosely at our sides. In a perfect position, you are perfectly balanced and perfectly still.

Once I'd learnt this, every pause on a London Underground platform, when the next train was three eternal minutes away and I was stood elbow to elbow with complete strangers, listening for the clatter, hum and squeal of the next train, I'd practise my perfect stillness. It was like transporting myself out of the noisy bowels of London, to a place of serenity. Sometimes I'd notice I was attracting the attention of some of my fellow commuters, which I found curious. Try it. It is curious.

When you try this, **colour** in the little person standing tall in your Ship's Log. Keep up with the thankfuls - you're doing great.

PAUSE
& REFLECT

Waterpot Walking

Waterpot Walking

Now that you can stand, can you walk? Probably not. Nor sit neither. According to Esther Gokhale, our omnipresent back problems of the Western world, are all do do with the fact we don't stand or walk properly. Apparently a lot of back pain and shoulder problems all boil down to bad posture. I read about her technique of good posture and looked at her illustrations of wrong and right.

The book resonated with me because at the time I was having physiotherapy - again - for a long-standing 'shoulder cuff' injury, which first appeared when playing volleyball in my twenties, (glamorous images of bikini clad Aussie babes bounce across the mind's eye - completely incorrect in my case), but the pain was currently preventing me from fastening my bra behind my back (far less glamorous especially as I'm no longer twenty).

Apparently our bodies are designed to balance upright with the vertebrae of our spine, stacked on top of each other like a tower of kiddies' wooden building bricks, and our invisible tails are free to wag rather than tucked in and sat on. In the book are pictures of women in African villages walking around with pots on their heads and in my mind's eye I could see the gentle, erect gait of a water-pot carrying woman. I could see the very particular arm position in gesticulating speech, where the arms seem to be attached further back on

Our bodies are designed to balance upright.

the body than mine and hang free to the elbow, with just the forearms and hands moving to illustrate a conversation (and none of the pain of a shoulder cuff injury).

The more I thought about it, the more it made sense: Imagine making a model person with a drinks bottle for the torso. When you pin the arms on the sides, they hang down the side of the body and swing freely. If they had to lift things up it would be easy.

If however, you made the model person using a curved banana for a torso and pinned the arms on the shoulders, the arms would hang down in front of the body, pulling forward from the shoulders. Lifting things would require more effort because their back would have to work, as well as their arm muscles. As Bananaman's spine is curved not stacked, his back is already pulling a load just from the weight of the arms when standing. Bingo, back pain is made.

Try this yourself - *stand up* and copy the water-bottle person's pose. Really feel your puppet string pulling up from the top of your head.

STRAIN!

It tends to change the position of your neck. Check yourself out in the mirror. Do you look taller? Is it easier to take slower, deeper breaths?

Roll your shoulders one at a time; Left shoulder forwards, up, over and back. Right shoulder forwards, up, over and back.

As you take a deep breath, can you feel yourself relaxing and feeling calmer? Now lift a big imaginary box in front of you, until it's level with your nose. Can you feel the difference in how your arms move and feel, now that your back is doing nothing?

Now gently **bring** your arms out to the side like a ballet dancer, and gently flap your wings like a bird. Does that feel different to normal?

Compare this with Bananaman:

Stand like Bananaman, with a curved back. To look forward you have to curve your neck up awkwardly. Now try lifting your huge box up, until it's level with your nose.

Can you feel the difference in effort from when you were a drinks bottle person? Your back has to work now.

Try the ballet dancer and bird.

Do you feel as graceful as before?

At school we had a gym teacher who liked to punish the whole class if someone was still talking when we'd been told to be quiet. 'Right ten squats everyone! Katy's talking'. It felt mean, but was so effective that it rarely needed repeating. As well as the squats and push ups, I remember the punishment of 'Hold your arms out to the side for five minutes!' This was an absolute killer. However years later, in a yoga class I was taught to stand tall like a puppet, and bring my arms up as if there were cushions of air lifting them up. I was astonished to find that I could have easily held this position, long enough to spite the teacher. What a shame I hadn't known that as a twelve year old.

Now you've found which back position gives you freer arm movement, and requires less effort for lifting, you can try walking around with a book on your head as Victorian schoolgirls were taught. You'll find that your head has to be in a very different position to normal. You can coil a tea-towel on your head first to counteract slippy hair.

You'll find that this posture; walking as if you have a pot of water on your head, is conducive to the deep breathing, but that scurrying around highly stressed, with a curved posture like a bananaman, isn't.

Get carrying that waterpot on your head, as well as the bottle in your bag.

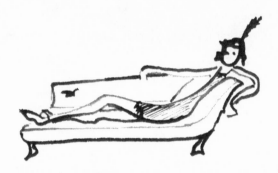

Gokhale tracks the history of bad posture, pointing out that Victorian pictures depict people sitting very upright. However pictures of the roaring 1920's show the couch and the slouch had appeared, as glamorous flappers reclined on chaise-longs, smoking cigarette extensions and sporting ostrich feathers in diamanté headbands. The same fashion can be seen in furniture if you think of old fashioned kitchen chairs, fireside chairs, and firmly stuffed chesterfield sofas, starkly contrasting our modern oversized, softly-stuffed sofas and huge circular cinema armchairs, all designed for slouching. Even car seats have followed the same progression, from sitting bolt upright in the early horse-less carriages, to reclining in modern, luxury cars.

Start noticing where and how you sit, and try practising Victorian sitting.

If you're petite you'll know that sofas tend to be made for giants! Simply leaning back on a sofa creates a slouch for petite people, the length of whose thigh bones, correspond perfectly with their height! Try packing some cushions in behind you or keep a look out for a kinder, more petite chair.

Like standing, water-pot walking can be practised anywhere, and it really adds interest to walking around. It can be quite a challenge in cold weather as you hold your head high, and it reminds me to wear a scarf. Having experimented, I know that the alternative, of tensing your body and hunching forward, frowning against the weather, does not actually make you feel warmer, or the wind calmer or the rain lighter. It does however make you feel like you're battling the elements. Makes you feel you're at war. Obviously a war you can't win; you against the elements. This is a negative outlook. However, standing tall, carrying your (invisible) water-pot on your head, (with a warm scarf around your neck), noticing the feel of the weather on your body, transforms the experience from a battle to a challenge ,and makes it enjoyable. Try it. Try walking your body as it was designed to be walked.

If you can stand still like you're standing in serenity, and walk water-pot tall, congratulations! You're transcending the mundane, and entering the plane of love.

When you try this, in your Ship's Log, *colour* in the little stick person with the pot on their head. Did you manage to colour in a waterpot today as well? Keep up the thankfuls. They're worth it and so are you.

PAUSE
& REFLECT

How Fit Is Your Face?

How Fit Is Your Face?

So now we can stand tall and look the world in the eye. This is the new you, who is actually the real you, looking the world in the eye. But what of your fitness?

During lockdown, having been ordered to stay in our homes or near our homes and having all our usual haunts shut, perhaps like me you found that your fitness levels decreased. One New Year I rather impulsively declared that I was going to run the London Marathon fifteen months later. (Don't panic, I'm not going to suggest this for you). I got a bit of a shock when a friend took me seriously and offered to join me following the NHS's Couch to 5k programme. There was nowhere really to go on this one, except to learn to keep my pipe dreams in my head. However the NHS Couch to 5k app is excellent and aims to get you running for 5k/30 mins non-stop in 12 weeks. At the end of the programme amazingly I was actually able to run for 30 minutes non-stop, although not fast enough to clock up 5k. After a few more weeks however I was able to run 5k (in 42 minutes in case you're wondering). Marrying the two, the 5k and the 30 minutes, still eludes me as did the London Marathon (because, fortunately for me, that year it was cancelled and off the hook I jumped).

Doing my 5k made me realise what a huge undertaking a twenty-six mile marathon would be. The difference between my 5k fitness, and the necessary twenty-six miles fitness, was enormous.

Obviously no one expects to run a marathon without intensively training their muscles first, and it's unsurprising your muscles complain about being stretched in new ways (mine certainly did). You understandably would have to build up your range of movement gradually, and your stamina slowly (I think the first run I did with the app was for only thirty seconds!), and gradually your muscles and fitness will build.

None of this will be news for you, but have you ever thought that the same goes for the muscles of your smile? If you're not used to smiling anymore, your smile muscles will struggle to form the shape of a full beam, or to have the endurance to keep it up. Do you remember laughing until your cheeks ached? That's your smile muscles. Let's start exercising them.

Over the page are some simple yoga exercises you can do to get your face mobile again, get your face out of its couch mode and back into life. Try these in the privacy of your own home because, warning, they do look rather odd! So let's go for it!

Smiles are highly contagious and grow quicker than the weeds in the lawn!

1) **Stretch** your mouth open as wide as you can as if you're trying to eat the biggest burger ever.

2) Next **widen** this into a Wallace and Grommet exaggerated grin as you close your mouth and stretch that as far as you can.

3) **Repeat** this burger + Wallace & Grommet Grin 10 times. If you do it in front of a mirror, you get the added benefit of laughing at yourself too!

4) Now you've got an idea of how far your mouth can stretch, **say** your vowels in an exaggerated, cartoon manner. A, e, i, o, u. Say this a few times.

5) Next **bare** your teeth like a bulldog, with your lower teeth in front of you upper teeth, like an exaggerated pout and push your chin out (yep, this one's worth shutting your eyes for). Hold for 5 seconds. Release. Hold for 5 seconds. Release. Hold for 5 seconds. Release (that's three sets in case I lost you)

6) Now you've done the ugly bit, **pucker up** for a big kiss. Then grin like you just got lucky! Repeat! Pucker, grin, pucker, grin, pucker, grin. (If you're like me, you'll find yourself livening up the action with silly noises too).

The first time you do this, your face with feel rather pulled, but keep practising every day and your face will soften. A good routine is that as you get out of bed, and your feet touch the floor each morning, do a few burger-Wallace & Grommet's, recite your vowels, add a few bulldog grimaces and a few big kisses. As you climb into bed at night, do the same.

That will sort out your suppleness. Next comes the workout, and as all good Fitness Trainers say, training should be enjoyable. Flick through your favourite TV channels, or Youtube, and find the stand up comedians. Start watching comedians and comedies instead of your normal TV. Find what makes you laugh. It could be nothing at first, but as your face becomes more supple and exercised, you'll find the laughs come easier too.

As you practise your smile, you will find smiles are highly contagious and grow quicker than the weeds in the lawn! Look out for opportunities to practise that smile.

Exercise:

1. *Make* a list of your favourite Stand-Up Comedians.

2. *Make* a list of your favourite comedies.

3. *Ask* your friends for their suggestions (my friend suggested the American sitcom 'Modern Family'. Turns out we love it and it has two hundred and fifty episodes to work through!)

When you've tried the exercises, *colour* in the little Wallace face in your Ship's Log. What else could you colour in on your Ship's Log today?

Don't forget to keep up the thankfuls. Some days they will really make you smile.

PAUSE
& REFLECT

Hug The World

Hug The World

Now that we're walking tall, looking the world in the eye, and have a smile at the ready, the world is ours to be had.

Ever noticed how the birds in the wildlife programmes stand tall, puff themselves up, strut their stuff and prance around in all their finery? Standing tall helps you feel more confident. There are other tricks too, which don't necessarily involve fanning out long feathers, but each to their own and I've always quite fancied some ostrich feathers to fan.

I was at a conference and the speaker stood up and beamed at us all. 'Welcome!' she cheered, throwing her arms wide. She proceeded to tell us her name, and the aims of the talk she was about to give, all the time holding her arms out in a wide embrace. The audience immediately warmed to her, enjoying the virtual hug she was giving.

The talk was all about 'self-care,' and the audience was full of stressed, strung out parents, but with the speaker's arms held wide, they visibly relaxed into her hug and basked in the warmth of her smile and personality. I noted how beautiful she looked, the lovely colours in which she was dressed, and felt the joy she exuded.

As her talk continued, and her arms remained wide, she drew attention to her spread arms, which surprisingly still didn't seem odd or out of place, despite being a contrast to the usual pose of a keynote speaker.

Have a smile at the ready, the world is ours to be had.

The speaker's name was Hil, and the impression she left on me was deep.

Hil explained that the reason she was holding her arms wide was to fill herself with the feeling of confidence, and that this simple exercise, of holding your arms wide for 5 minutes every morning, was all it took to lighten your day, and give you the energy to embrace the day, whatever challenges you may need to face.

Try it. **Beam and smile**. Open your arms out wide to hug the world.

It's proven that your can use your body to bring about positive changes. This is the basis of a therapy called CBT (Cognitive Behaviour Therapy), which works on the basis that your thoughts, feelings and actions are all connected, and by changing one element, you can impact the other two elements. I.e you feel miserable, you slouch on the sofa, you think what a lonely, friendless person you are. Any one of those elements could have come first, and you're on a spiral downwards.

However you can also make a change to just one of those elements, which will then impact the others. I.e you feel miserable, you get off the

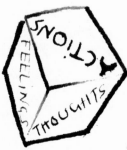

sofa, and force yourself to go out for a walk in nature. Once in nature your thought patterns begin to change, (you wonder if that mushroom is edible, you think how a flask of hot chocolate would be welcome) and lo and behold, your feelings have changed, you're not miserable anymore.

So proof enough to give it a try.

Open your arms to the wonders of the world, catch all the love that's out there.

Draw a little stick person in your Ship's Log as you catch the love. Have you managed to colour in more than one thing a day on your Ship's Log? Try standing tall now. That's two things today already. Well done you!

Keep up the thankfuls. Bright things are out there for the finding.

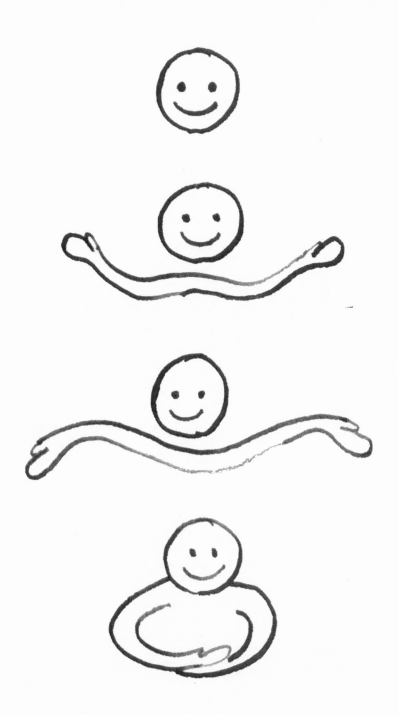

PAUSE
& REFLECT

Sky On Your Head

Sky On Your Head

Today I'm going to give you a a new language. I believe language is important for focussing. If you were aiming to go to the city of Edinburgh, you would be far more likely to get there, if you knew its name was Edinburgh. Vocabulary works as a shorthand for communication and thinking. You don't have to describe the city in detail to identify it, you just have to name it. It's called Edinburgh.

If I was going to call anything my personal cure all, this would be it: Sky On Your Head. Get some Sky On Your Head.

That's it. It's one of those basic human needs that has been forgotten in our rush for progress. We all need some sky on our head. People pay a fortune to get a nice bit of sky on their head, but they call it something else; they couple it with mountain under their feet and call it hiking; or a cruise ship under their derriere and call it a cruising, but what they're actually buying is sky on their head, which if you stop to think about it, is freely available everywhere. We rush, rush, rush. In and out of houses, and cars, and workplaces, and shops, only stopping to get sky on our heads when it's time for annual holidays. Then we often climb into an aeroplane, in order to get out underneath a different bit of sky, and think how wonderful it is. When on holiday we can't get enough of sky on our heads.

If I was going to
call anything my personal cure,
this would be it: Sky On Your Head.

Northumberland in Northern England is known as the county of 'big skies' but even tiny skies are good for the soul. I have always been struck by the title of Christine Marion Fraser's memoirs, 'Blue Above the Chimneys'. Growing up in urban poverty, in an industrial city, the little patch of sky above the chimneys dominating her view, was a symbol of hope for her. Her observation reminds me that there is sky everywhere, but sometimes we have to look hard to find our quota. It's always worth the effort though.

Go get some Sky On Your Head. That's your task for the day. Go claim your bit of sky. Wherever you live, go outside, get some Sky On Your Head.

Evie hasn't been outside the entire lockdown. She has fragile health and had been shielding. For her it was hard to get some sky on her head, but it can be done gradually, little step, by little step. She could start by simply standing in front of a window and opening it, feeling the change in temperature, and breathing in some fresh air. The next step could be to stick her head out the window, and catch some sky on her head. She will need to be patient and go a little bit further, and stay out a little bit longer, each day. One step at a time.

First she may just open the door, step out and stand on the door step for a few minutes. The day after that she may be able to get all the way to her front gate, and pause to look up at the sky before returning inside. The next day she can try and go a little bit further. Then the next day a bit further more, and keep at it until gradually she's built up her time outside, got a little bit more sky on her head each day, and a little bit farther away from home.

The psychological term for this is Graded Exposure. It works. You just have to change your expectations. Focus on what you can do, not can't do. Accept that progress can be slow but that even an extra metre, or an extra minute, is all travelling in the right direction. The point is to persist, to keep trying, to keep gently pushing your boundaries.

To pause before returning home is good. It gives you time to register your achievement, to realise that you can do it. When you have Sky On Your Head, feel the sun, the rain, the breeze. It'll be there however much mankind has tried to deny it. If it's sunny, say to yourself 'thank you for the light and warmth,' and catch some sun on your face.

If it's raining, say 'thank you for my waterproof clothing,' and notice which bits of you are wet. Is your nose wet? Or your hands? Your hair, or your knees? If you've been caught in the rain and soaked to the skin, say 'thank you that there is shelter for me nearby' whether you've returned home, or found shelter under a tree, or in a doorway. If it's windy say 'thank you for the wind that blows the clouds and brings changes to the weather'. And next time, remember the old saying: 'There's no such thing as bad weather, just inappropriate clothing'.

Everyday, get some Sky On Your Head. Even if it's only for a minute. Stand on your doorstep and pause. Look up. Claim your bit of sky. Notice the weather. Venture a little further each day. Where can you go that's new? What can you see that's different?

Look for more opportunities to get Sky On Your Head. Manage your transport to get some more Sky On Your Head. Park your car a bit further away from your destination, so you have to walk. I've found that the time it takes to find nearby parking spaces, is about the same or more, than the extra walking time you give yourself by parking father away. Or get on the bus one stop further down the road and get off it one stop earlier. In London, I found if I got off the tube a bit earlier, and walked the last bit to work, I'd avoid the rush, and bustle, and horrid lighting of the underground walkways, not to mention the rather indirect route. Instead, I'd see life and vibrancy, and interesting architecture, and benefit from sky on my head.

Even better, take a bike journey. If you have cycle paths near you, it can be very satisfying to nip and weave, and beat the traffic by using bike paths. You can even get electric bikes now which supplement your peddling with a bit of electric power, although personally I find that after about three journeys, my bike muscles begin to rapidly tone up. It does always take a few journeys though, because my bike muscles obviously aren't used for much else.

Think about where in your daily life you can build in Sky On Your Head time.

At lunchtime? Instead of a sandwich at your desk, or going out, only to go into a cafe or shop, go seeking Sky On Your Head places. I've been amazed to find pocket parks nearby my place of work in town. In some cities I've lived in, I've managed to sneak up onto the roof with my box of sandwiches and join the pigeons in their world.

The sky is always there. When you're out, look up.

- What kind of sky can you see?

- Can you see the sun?

- The colour of the clouds, the movement of the wind, the shape of the weather to come?

Now look down.

- Can you see the sky on the ground?

- The shape of the shadows cast by the sun, or the movement of small things blown by the wind?

- When it rains can you see the impact of raindrops, hitting the pavement or puddles?

- What shape are the clouds today?

- What colour is the sky? If you stare at a fixed point and watch the clouds about it, which way are the clouds travelling?

- Which way is east, where the sun rises?

- Where is west, where the sun sets?

- Where is south, where the sun hangs out in the Northern hemisphere?

- What is touching the sky?

- Does the sky, shape the landscape, or does the landscape shape the sky, like Christine Marion Fraser's?

Sky On Your Head will make you feel good. Many of us now have step counters counting our steps, monitoring our heart beat, and recording the amount of time we spend in aerobic exercise, but what if you had a Sky On Your Head counter? How many minutes today? How many minutes tomorrow?

Getting three children up, washed, dressed, out the door, into the car, seat belts on, book-bags in hand, and into school on time, used to be my venture into hell. Until that is, I swapped to walking to school, despite it being a mile and a half away. We had to leave home thirty minutes earlier, however the journey to school was transformed from a chore into a delight. The walk to school was full of chats, and play, and skipping, and admiring icy puddles, or flocking birds. The school run became a wonderful time and fun for everyone, and the extra time it took, was there already: We already got up early in the morning due to natural earlier risers, and having less time to get out of the door, actually meant that everyone just had to get up, and get on at a steady pace, with no big bits of spare time to get engrossed in something else, that would be

Sky On Your Head will make you feel good.

hard to be dragged away from.

Once we were all out the door, we were all in fun time, unlike when I was in charge of driving the car, and the kids alone were looking to find fun. We all benefited from sky on our heads, lots of Vitamin D and a physical workout. The walk also proved to be a nice long transition between home and school and calmed the child who found transitions difficult. We all had time to practise spelling homework which had been forgotten, and times tables which should've been learnt. The child who wanted exclusive-mummy time for a chat had this uninterrupted, whilst the other two ran, or played, or chatted together. It really was a win-win.

It rarely rained and even when it did, it never lasted long, and gave us the benefit of being thankful we were staying dry, or that we could escape the rain once in school. Walking through different weather and seasons, meant we noticed the changes, that each day is precious. We were really living. Instead of a morning of misery and torture, we had fun and adventures. Later on you'll understand what I mean when I say the clouds lifted from my clock segment, and were replaced by sunshine yellow. My brisk walk home took half the time, stretched my legs and I enjoyed either the wind whistling through my ears or twenty-two long minutes of my own uninterrupted thoughts, with nothing to do except put one foot in front of the other.

There is always sky. Life is good.

When you get some Sky On Your Head, *colour* in the sun in your Ships Log.

If you're a complete beginner at Sky On Your Head, note down the minutes (or seconds) you had Sky On Your Head, and congratulate yourself every time you get some. You're travelling in the right direction!

Now I have some science to back up my obsession with Sky On Your Head, and there's rather a lot of it, so, if you fancy a deeper dive into the benefits, read on. If not, see you in the next chapter about spring cleaning.

1. One byproduct of seeking Sky On Your Head is exercise. Exercise is beneficial for maintaining health.

2. Exercise also reduces inflammation, and inflammation in the brain is thought to be a contributory factor of depression.

3. Sky On Your Head also counteracts 'SAD' Syndrome: Seasonal Affected Disorder was eventually recognised in the 1980s, and just gave a name to what most of us knew anyway; that a lack daylight in winter can give you the winter-blues.

In winter when we might not be getting enough daylight, our biological rhythms can be thrown out of sync, which can lead to the kind of symptoms that characterise SAD:

- sleep problems
- lethargy
- over-eating
- depression
- loss of libido
- mood changes.
- social problems (including irritability and desire to avoid social contact)
- anxiety (including tension and inability to tolerate stress)

Treatments recommended by the SAD Association, include getting out for thirty minutes walk in the morning and having breakfast by a window. Sounds awfully like Sky On Your Head doesn't it?

BBC's Dr Michael Mosely's investigations also identified symptoms of cravings for sugary carbohydrates and weight-gain (anyone else see a relationship there?)

Brain scans by Dr Brenda McMahon of Copenhagen University Hospital revealed that in winter, the brains of SAD suffers appear to be being deprived of serotonin, a brain chemical linked to feelings of well-being and happiness. I rest my case!

4. Sky On Your Head tops up your Vitamin D. The body creates vitamin D from direct sunlight on our skin. However if we don't go outdoors, or it's a British winter, the medical recommendation is to take a Vitamin D supplement of ten micrograms (NHS England). Vitamin D is essential for healthy bones, teeth and muscle. A lack of Vitamin D can cause bone deformities in children, and a thinning of the bones in adults. Vitamin D also has a role in reducing inflammation. This ties in with the evidence linking inflammation of the brain to low mood.

5. By seeking Sky On Your Head you are avoiding electric lights on your head. I was surprised to learn that sensitivity to fluorescent lights is common amongst people who are diagnosed with dyslexia, Autism, ADHD, and epilepsy, due to underlying visual processing issues. Occupational

Therapists can carry out Sensory Assessments to identify these and any other sensory issues. Fluorescent strip lighting can cause headaches, stomach aches and a generalised feeling of being unwell. As strip lights are in much public transport, many workplaces, and also home kitchens, just escaping it can make you feel better, even before all the benefits of Sky On Your Head hit you.

Exercise:

Go out, get some Sky On Your Head and colour in the little sun symbol on your Ships Log. Or better still, write an estimate of the total number of minutes you spend getting Sky On Your Head. Even if it was only one minute standing on your doorstep. Tomorrow it may be two minutes.

For the next seven days focus on getting some Sky On Your Head. As you do this, notice anything new. It could be that you're practising your Waterpot Walking and it's becoming more natural. Or perhaps you're feeling on the right side of coping. Perhaps, before you've gone for a walk, you've held your arms out and hugged the world, so that when you met people, you felt more confident to practise smiling at them?

And still I cheer you on, with 'keep up the thankfuls!' Have any of them been about the wonders of nature yet? Have you been able to colour in three things a day on your Ship's Log yet? When you do, you'll know you're definitely heading for fairer waters.

PAUSE
& REFLECT

Spring Clean Your Lungs

Spring Clean Your Lungs

Now that we've practised standing, walking tall, hugging the world, getting some Sky On Your Head, and our Ship's Log is filling up, I'm going to talk to you about breathing. Yes, if you're living you're breathing, but did you know that we have several parts of our lungs, and we only usually use the upper-parts, exchanging the air only in the top of our lungs? The air in the bottom of our lungs rarely gets changed. But it needs to be changed. Just like our houses need to be regularly vacuumed and mopped. We change this air by straightening our backs, to get all our airways straightened out (lying down or standing up). Then we breathe in deep and slow: Breathe in through your nose, pause, and out through your mouth.

This is how we check that we're actually pulling fresh air, deep into our lungs: Put your hand on your tummy, just above your tummy button. This is over your diaphragm, a big muscle that contracts to pull air down into your lungs. Now take a long, slow deep breath in, and if you feel your hand rising on your tummy, then your diaphragm is working and pulling a big breath down deep into your lungs.

When we then breathe out, we're getting rid of all that stale old air ready to replace it with fresh clean air. Obviously if this was air from a mountain top, that would be super-great, but even new city air is better than old city air. There's a huge scale of air quality ranging from sucking a car's exhaust pipe, right up to savouring the air from the top of a remote hill, where all the frilly lichen grows on the tree branches, vouching for the lack of pollution (lichens require very clean air and the frilly ones require very, very clean air).

Polluted air isn't limited to roadsides; Many new products we put in our homes can give off subtle fumes that are now known to irritate our lungs (this is called off-gassing and why some sensitive people don't like the smell of some new household items). Perfumed air fresheners, (i.e the plug in ones) and some perfumes commonly used in household products/cleaners, can trigger asthma. That's why getting outside and deep breathing is so important. Deep breathing whilst getting some Sky On Your Head is a win win.

The fact that 60% of people with asthma say perfume is a trigger, and that according to asthma.org.uk, one in eleven people have asthma, perfumes are obviously a big problem.

Coming from a family with asthmatics, I'm reminded of the canaries that used to be lowered in cages down coal mines to test the safety of the air, before the workers went down themselves. If the canary stopped singing, and the cage was hoisted back up with a dead canary inside it, it meant there were dangerous gases in the coal mine. Too dangerous to send humans into. I think asthmatics are the human canaries: If asthmatics near you are struggling with the local air quality, take heed. It means there is a big problem with the quality of the air, even if your body isn't registering it for you.

Therefore when you are taking your deep breaths and filling your lungs up with new air, remember the canaries. The farther from the man-made world you can go, and the deeper into the natural world you can get, the better.

Much as we may love to, it's not easy to access that lovely fresh air on a mountain top, so start by just trying to go one better than you currently are: If you're in your bedroom, open your window and stand in front of it. If you're in your living room, open your front door and stand in front of it. If you're out, find a patch of green park to stand in. If you're in a park, find a quiet tree to stand under.

Let me show you how to take five deep breaths by drawing around the outline of one hand with the index finger of the other hand, just like you drew round your hand with a crayon when you were a child.

Exercise:

1. ***Breathe in*** through your nose, as you trace your drawing finger up the side of your thumb. Pause at the top, then breathe out through your mouth, as you trace your finger down the inside of your thumb.

2. ***Breathe in*** through your nose, as you trace your finger up the side of your index finger and stop, pausing at the top. Breathe out through your mouth, as you trace your finger down the other side of your index finger.

3. ***Breathe in*** through your nose, as you trace your finger up the side of your middle finger, pause, breathe out through your mouth, as you trace down your middle finger.

4. ***Breathe in*** through your nose, as you trace up the side of your ring finger, pause at the tip, breathe out through your mouth, as you trace down the side of your ring finger.

5. ***Breathe in*** through your nose, as you trace up the side of your little pinkie finger, pause, breathe out through your mouth as you trace down it.

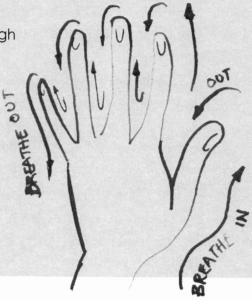

You've just given yourself a high-five!

Anytime, anywhere. Wherever you can. You have to wait for a bus? Count your high-five. Waiting at the checkout? Count your high-five. At those times you'd normally pull out your phone to pass the time? Count your high-five.

High-five. Congratulate yourself. You have just found the time to have a little spring clean of your lungs. Anytime you can. Anywhere you can. This is living. This is energy. This is slowing the Waltzer of life.

At the worst times of my life, the world was in perpetual motion. I was so exhausted I wanted to rest, but sleep never gave me that rest. I just wanted the world to stop. But it never did. It just raced more.

I needed to stand on a mountain top and breathe. Or even just breathe. How about imagining a mountain top, whilst you just breathe?

I'm breathing in the view now. Are you? I can see a vast sky above my head, and beneath my feet the land falls away, with clouds tumbling down the mountain sides, giving glimpses of what lies below. I am counting out my high-five.

Practise breathing because it's something that's unconscious, that has been knocked off kilter in our fast, fast, world. It needs practice to reset it and to establish a new pattern of behaviour. Most of us have been breathing so wrong, for so long, that we can't even remember how to do it properly.

Whenever you feel yourself winding up and getting stressed, go for the high-five. And when you've done it, I'll be there high-fiving you.

When you've tried this, draw a little hand in your Ship's Log (as you draw a hand you'll find out why cartoonists tend to draw only three fingers and a thumb - four fingers are a bit of a squash!).

How many things have you coloured in in your Ship's Log today? Keep up the thankfuls. Do they feel good yet?

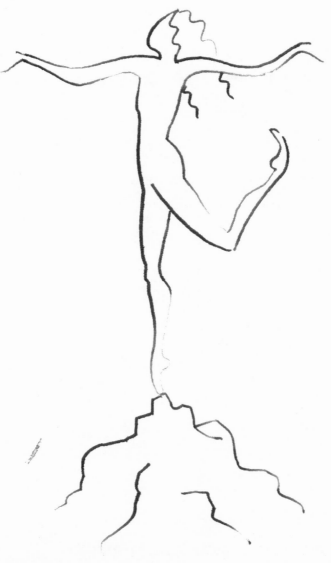

Get into Your Body Takeaways

This chapter has been all about starting to live intentionally. Starting to take control of your life. You may have heard the phrase 'being intentional' before, but this is what it really means. You are now choosing how you are living your life. These are tiny little changes, tiny little upgrades, but they will all take you spiralling upwards. Slowly at first, but things can get better really fast, so hold tight for a thrilling ride!

We learnt how to stand tall, do water pot walking, get our faces fit, hug the world, seek out Sky On Your Head, and spring clean our lungs.

Make a note here of things that struck a chord / things that worked really well for you, things you want to remember or use for your Life Manual.

PAUSE
& REFLECT

Chapter Three
Get Out of Your Head

When The Only Way Is Up

When The Only Way Is Up

The one benefit of hitting rock bottom, is that when the only way is up, you've got to make changes. Paul McKenna, the hypnotist, suggested that each day we should look for something beautiful, something wonderful, something to be thankful for. The man is so right, and those three things are what got me spiralling back up, at a time when tickets out of here were tempting.

Beautiful, Wonderful, Thankful. BWT. It's an exercise in positivity, an expansion of your morning gratitudes, and an exercise that can last all day. Hopefully by this point, you've managed to complete seven days of gratitudes, and have filled in seven hearts on your Ship's Log. If the days weren't consecutive, don't worry, that bit comes with practice. My days were awfully hit and miss at first, now it's an effortless way of life.

So what is beautiful? Beautiful could be as simple as seeing a colour you like. Sometimes you have to scour your landscape, scour what you see. Sometimes, it can take all day to find that 'something beautiful'. Remember to look. When you look, you will find. The looking and the finding will be creating new pathways of positivity in your brain. You will be making good use of your brain's plasticity (that I talked about in 'A New Brain') and you'll be rewiring your brain the way you want it, so that you can experience a happy joyful life.

When the only way is up, you've got to make changes.

Wonderful can be anything you like. For me it might be that daisy, growing through a crack in the pavement, or it might be a snippet of music drifting from a soulful busker, or catching sight of a Skylark, oft heard out in the fields near me, but rarely seen. Examine the definition of wonderful to broaden your field.

The dictionary defines wonderful as: inspiring delight; inspiring pleasure; inspiring admiration; something that's extremely good; something marvellous. So it could be, the softness of a flower petal, or a piece of velvet, the waft of someone's cooking, or passing perfume. Wonderful will always be there, but you have to actively seek, until recognising wonderful becomes second nature. Wonderful could be a sight, a sound, a smell, a taste, a touch.

Think of a wonderful? I have a smooth stone from the beach in a coat pocket. I always love it when I re-find it. Which of your senses is most likely to delight you?

Exercise:

Circle below the sense that is most likely to delight you.

Touch	Hearing	Spacial Awareness (proprioception)
Taste	Movement (kinaesthesia)	
Smell		Temperature (thermoception)
Sight	Balance (equilibrioception)	

I heard an interview with the perfumer, Jo Malone, and she spoke of the fragrances of her childhood. Obviously she has an exceptional sense of smell, and it is core to who she is, and her life. Hearing Jo Malone made me realise that we all have different strengths in our senses, but because our education system doesn't value these, we are often unaware of how exceptional we all are.

Think for a moment, which of your senses are more exceptional? *Write* it here...

I can't balance flavours in cooking, so I suspect my sense of taste isn't that strong, but I can sense the emotions in a room full of people, even if they've just left.

Which one of your senses, are you most likely to use to find your wonderful? *Write* it here...

We are often unaware of how exceptional we all are.

What is thankful? Something to be thankful for is always possible, but at times when this is hard, go back to your basic needs. Do you have enough food, water and shelter? Is the sun shining, or the rain watering the crops for us? These are the simplest things to be thankful for. Be thankful for your haves, not your nots. Don't be thankful that it's not raining, be thankful instead for the positive, that's it's a dry day. See the cheese, not the holes as Tom's mate Jerry would say (ok, I made that up. I don't think he even talked did he? But you get the idea).

If ever you are crushed by fear and anxiety, flip your fears to find something to be thankful for; A glass half empty is also half full. For instance if you're worried your loved one might get seriously ill, flip it and say "I'm thankful for the health my loved one has got". If you don't have enough money to pay the bills today, flip it and say "I'm thankful I have food in my belly and a roof over my head tonight". If you don't have enough food in your cupboards, say "I'm thankful that the farmers here are able to grow enough food".

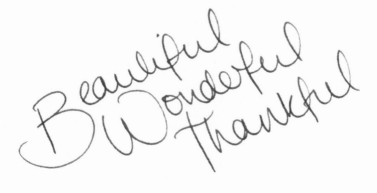

Beautiful
Wonderful
Thankful

Such thankfuls, help to remind us that we only have to be thankful for what we have at this precise moment in time. Today is today. Tomorrow is yet to come. This is practising positivity, this is living in love.

What fear could you flip to be a thankful? **Write** it here...

Fear   *Thankful*

Shall I tell you another story? Are you sitting comfortably? Then I'll begin.

Once upon a time I was served with an eviction notice, because my landlord had been pocketing the rent money, instead of paying his mortgage for the house he was renting out to me. I was given 14 days to get myself and family out. This was scary stuff. I had to force myself to be thankful that I had a roof over my head for the next two weeks. I had to work really hard on my thoughts though, to avoid borrowing from tomorrow's troubles. It is so easy to succumb to the emotions of fear, and I have found that decisions made through fear, tend to be bad decisions. Being thankful for what you have, helps you stay calm and objective, instead of getting lost in emotions. When you practise being thankful, you are able to see the whole situation more clearly, and use your logic to assess it.

*Avoid borrowing
from tomorrow's troubles.*

When I let my mind wander, and borrow from the worries of fourteen days' time, what I was doing was time-travelling to day fourteen, and experiencing the fear of being forcibly evicted by aggressive bailiffs. Why would anyone in their right mind, use their imagination to put themselves into the middle of a horror film? Why would anyone want to experience the emotions of bailiffs banging on their door, throwing their furniture out of the window, and locking them out of their home? But this is exactly what my mind was trying to do, straining like a dog on a leash, to think scary things.

In the scenario above I hadn't contacted any friends, so I didn't know who could give us a bed for the night. I was frightened of having to sleep on the street with my kids. I was fearful that I couldn't carry all my possessions under my arm, and that I would have to leave them on the roadside to be stolen, or rained on, and basically lost forever.

With these thoughts running through my head, understandably I'd be terrified. My palms would be sweating, my heart would be pumping blood into my arms and legs ready to fight the beast, or run from the beast. My capacity for calm logical thought and reasoning, would be shut down by my body, because my body would be filled with adrenaline in flight or fight mode.

My body's priority right at that moment, would be to run from the stampeding Woolly Mammoths, or to fight the Sabre Tooth tiger. My body would be prioritising muscle power, not brain power. However, because I knew I wanted to stay in control of the situation, I instead consciously tried to focus my thoughts on being thankful that I had a roof over my head, for the next thirteen nights.

So my adrenaline wasn't pumping, and my heart wasn't pounding, and my legs were not twitching. I wasn't preparing to outrun that Sabre Tooth Tiger. I was capable of calm logical thoughts. I was able to research where to get appropriate advice about my rights in this situation, and make an appointment with an adviser. I was able to contact rental agencies, to see what other properties might be available. I was able to tell my friends about my housing needs, and ask if they knew of any short term emergency lets, like holiday homes. I started doing that decluttering that I'd had always meant to do.

Thirteen days later, I moved my stuff into storage, and my family into an empty holiday cottage. We got through it.

Exercise: Now this moment:

What can you find to be your beautiful, your wonderful and your thankful? Hopefully you've already found three thankfuls this morning, so now you'll have to find a fourth!

Beautiful:

Wonderful:

Thankful:

In your Ship's Log, draw a little Beautiful, Wonderful, Thankful (BWT). Far more satisfying than a BLT.

Anything else to add to your Ship's Log for today?

PAUSE
& REFLECT

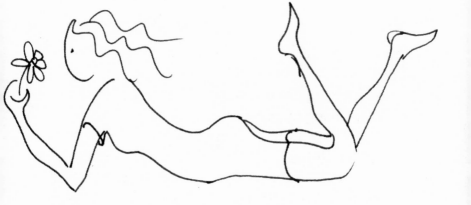

Living Without Stress

Living Without Stress

In the last chapter I told you about a stressful situation that happened to me, and how seeking out something beautiful, something wonderful and something to be thankful for, helped me to turn away from the fear of a particular event. However, a factor of 21st Century living, is that rather than there being one occasional stressful event that we have to navigate, many people are finding their whole lives are stressful, in every area, of every day.

There is therefore a lot of talk about stress levels, and people saying they want to de-stress, or be less stressed, or to avoid being stressed. What if we try our flip trick? Instead of aiming to have less of a bad thing, why not instead aim to have more of a good thing? Instead of having less stress, let's have more of its opposite. Doesn't that sound wonderful? Surely the opposite of stressed, has to be something nice? However we don't seem to have specific, agreed vocabulary for this opposite. We only see stress, or the absence of stress.

What happens when we aim for less? Let's say we aim to eat less cake (I'm on the same page as Charlie Macksey's mole on this one). What seems to happen, is we start obsessing about not eating cake, and

Instead of aiming to have less of a bad thing, why not instead aim to have more of a good thing?

in my case I know I'll actually consume more cake than I otherwise would.

But, what if it was darkness we wanted less of? That's an easier one to naturally flip isn't it? We'd find it easy to aim for more light. We'd aim to get a torch, or a new lamp, or a brighter light bulb. We'd naturally focus on the light we wanted, and not the dark we didn't want.

However with the emotionally loaded things like cake (or is that just me...?), we have a tendency to focus on the negative, the 'not', the 'not eat anymore cake'. The result being, we end up actually attracting more of what we don't want; every corner, every cafe, everywhere, will suddenly be selling delicious coffee cake. So my point is (if you can get past the visions I'm implanting in your brain of all that scrumptious cake), that if we want to de-stress, or have less stress, we need to focus on the opposite of stress, and aim for that. Forget worrying about the stress, and start aiming for its opposite. But what is the opposite to stress?

According to Dr David Hamilton, a scientist and author of many books, in hormone terms, there is an opposite of being stressed. So, to find the vocabulary we require, we just have to follow the hormones:

The hormones we release when we're stressed, are Adrenalin and Cortisol. Great for fleeing from the Sabre Tooth Tiger to the safety of our cave, but in the context of the 21st century living, stress isn't a short lived event but a constant state. A constant state of stress causes all these things:

- Increases blood pressure (high blood pressure creates a risk of heart attack)

- Damages the cardiovascular system (the heart and blood vessels)

- Suppresses the immune system (which should be fighting disease)

- Tenses the nervous system (making muscles tighten)

- Increases inflammation (shown to cause joint problems)

- Can trigger depression

Interestingly there's a hormone that does the exact opposite to all these things. A hormone which:

- Reduces blood pressure

- Protects the cardiovascular system

- Boosts the immune system

- Relaxes the nervous system

- Reduces inflammation

- Makes people happy

- Can be an antidote to depression

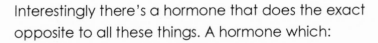

Drumroll please for the big reveal: This hormone is called Oxytocin. A naturally occurring chemical, produced in our brains. So instead of us focusing on trying to have less stress, or less Cortisol, or less Adrenaline, we can actually focus on having more of its opposite; more Oxytocin. If we fill our bodies with Oxytocin, this by its nature, will prevent us from being stressed. Sounds great doesn't it? So how do we get it?

As I said before, there's this wonderful trio of thoughts, feelings, and actions, and there are certain <u>actions</u> you can do, that will significantly increase your Oxytocin levels. There are also <u>thoughts</u>, that will increase your Oxytocin levels, and <u>feelings</u>, that will increase your Oxytocin levels too.

By now you may be wondering if increasing Oxytocin levels requires as much effort as it does to get a 'Runner's High' (which is the release of endorphins after intense exercise).

Fortunately Oxytocin is far easier to get. Oxytocin is known as the Hug-drug, or love drug, or the cuddle-chemical, and it's what our bodies produce when we're hugging, feeling love, making love, breast-feeding, and perhaps easiest of all (as no breasts or genitals are required), when we're being

kind. How simple is that? We just have to be kind.

So the opposite of Cortisol is Oxytocin and the opposite of stress is actually kindness. Dr David Hamilton also states (and he's a rather clever chap), that regardless of whether you do an act of kindness, receive an act of kindness or witness an act of kindness, the positive results for you, will be the same. Oxytocin!

Therefore if you want the world to be a better place, the ball is in your court, the power is in your heart. Don't wait for someone to be kind to you. Start the ball rolling by doing acts of kindness, and banish your stress in the process.

Exercise:

Make a list here of five things you can easily and effortlessly do, to get yourself an Oxytocin hit.

When you get that Oxytocin hit, **colour** in the happy pill in your Ship's Log.

And don't forget to keep practising your thankfuls. Or filling in your Ship's Log.

The opposite of stress is actually kindness.

If you want the world to be a better place, the ball is in your court, the power is in your heart.

oxytocin

me!

PAUSE
& REFLECT

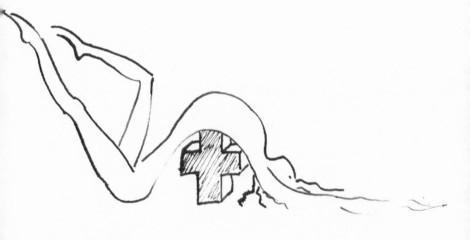

Surround Yourself With Positivity

Surround Yourself With Positivity

So if you are recognising beauty, wonder and gratitude, you're pumping up your body with the love drug oxytocin, what next?

Well, the famous motivational coach Jim Rohn says, "You are the average of the five people you spend the most time with." So look at who you are spending most time with, and think what the 'average' of them is. Is it who you want to be?

If you want to move forward in positivity, you need to surround yourself with positive people. Sounds obvious when you put it that way doesn't it? If you want to be a millionaire, wouldn't it be far easier, if you were surrounded by millionaires? So if you want be positive, surround yourself with positivity. Seek it out wherever you can. Keep moving on past negativity. Keep looking for positivity until you find it. If something doesn't feel right, then it isn't. That's your feelings talking to you. Listen to them.

We can all choose to live in positivity. It sounds harsh, but positivity isn't the privilege of the privileged. It's a mindset thing, and although we don't all have the same starting point, or inbuilt neurological pathways, it is something we can all choose to head for. We are creatures of free will.

Who are the people in your social group/family/workplace that you spend a lot of time with? Do any come to mind who seem to fill you with energy? Or any who seem to suck the lifeblood from your soul, an emotional vampire?

It's important you recognise these differences, so that with this awareness, you can make conscious choices about who you spend your time with, or how much time you spend with certain people.

I have one friend who regardless of how well or badly she's doing, always fills me with optimism and energy. So much so, that one time I felt compelled to draw her how I see her, because it contrasted how she saw herself at that moment. Whereas another friend always leaves me feeling, flat, drained and deflated. It's like one brings me rose tinted spectacles, and the other brings grey tinted specs. Both are decent people, but their effect on my energy levels is very different. Other friends are more middle ground.

You are the average of the five people you spend the most time with. - Jim Rohn

143

Exercise:

List who immediately springs to mind as a balloon person, and who as a drain person?

 Who *lifts* your energy up?

Who *drains* your energy out?

In my experience the closer you live to negativity, the more it drags you down, be it a person you share your home with, or a colleague you share your workplace with.

Negative people leave you feeling flat. They can find plenty of evidence to support their negative views, and find people, or things to lay blame on, and justify their decisions to not take any action to improve their situation. However, each of us can choose our viewpoint, our perspective, our glass half empty, or our glass half full. I'm not saying dump everyone who's feeling a bit glum, I'm saying look after you, as if you are a precious object, as if your energy levels are a burning life force to be nurtured and expanded, not diminished and extinguished.

Indigo Violet is feeling a bit flat today ...and a bit blue....

Your spark, the bit that's really you, needs to be nurtured to grow and burn brightly.

Have you ever lit a fire with tiny twigs and little sticks? Think how important it is to nurture that tiny spark of fire to become a burning flame. You'd protect it from cold blasts and from cold showers. In fact the survivalist Ray Mears, actually holds the first tiny flames in his cupped hands, to nurture and grow them. Your spark, the bit of you that's really you, needs to be cupped gently in your hands, and nurtured to grow, and shine, and light your life, to show you your way.

"When your problems are enormous it's the littlest things that get you moving" - Mel Robbins, author.

The littlest thing could be spending an extra five minutes a day in positivity, or five minutes less with negativity.

Exercise: The Sunshine Clock

You'll need some sunny colours for this, either pencil crayons or highlighter pens.

Below are two clocks. One to represent daytime 6am - 6pm and the other to represent nighttime 6pm - 6am

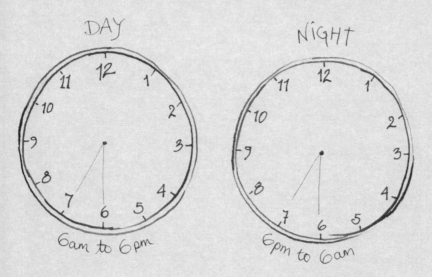

1. **Divide** each clock into segments representing the hours of the day in which you spend time with specific people. This could be 7am - 8.30am = family, 8.30am - 9am = local bus, 9am -12pm office etc.

2. **Colour** any sections that feel positive, due to the people in them, with a sunshine yellow crayon. The sections which feel negative, due the negativity of the people in them, colour these with your darkest crayon. Chose dark or sunny colours for all the other segments as befits.

3. **Review**: Take a moment to look at the colours of your two clocks.

4. **Write** down the answers to these questions:

How many sunshine hours each day do you have?

How many gloomy hours?

What colour is your alone time?

If your clocks look thunderous, it's time to brighten up your circle, literally. From now on, your alone time is going to get brighter.

5. **List** which other segments need brightening.

6. **List** which of your segments are the easiest to change?

7. **Make** an action plan for the easiest changes first. The rest can wait their turn.

My commuting segment used to be rather dark, as I find driving monotonous, until I made the decision that the journey would be 'me time', and organised some audio books to listen to. Maybe you have a journey each day that is monotonous. What could you do, to turn it into sunshine yellow? Could you make your journey a thing to look forward to, by intentionally selecting some favourite podcasts, or good books to accompany you? What could you do immediately, to turn on the sunshine?

Once you decide to make a tiny change, to pick up your yellow crayon and give your grey segments a new lease of life, you'll find these chores or drudges cease to be draining, and instead become fun. A time to look forward to. So keep and eye out for tiny changes you can make in your life, to get the yellow crayon working.

What can you do
to turn on the sunshine?

8. **Create** a life of sunshine yellow: Use the new clocks below to colour in the yellow bits of your current life. Now there are only good bits in your life, and bits you are making better.

My life in sunshine yellow

my life in sunshine yellow

9. **Think** what are the new things you're going to do to create a life of sunshine yellow?

10. **Write** these decisions around the edge of the clock, with arrows pointing to which segments your decisions will turn yellow.

11. **List** any preparations required (i.e loading up your phone with podcasts).

12. **Photocopy** this the clock pages and display it somewhere prominent. When you achieve a new yellow segment, colour it in and pat yourself on the back! Well done.

I love it!

Take a tiny step to live in positivity, and colour in a positive plus sign in your Ship's Log. What else have you been colouring in on your Ship's Log? How are the thankfuls going?

PAUSE
& REFLECT

On The Job

On The Job

What colour was your 9-5? If your job is a grey segment, grab the yellow crayon, hold it in your hand and think what tiny changes you can make to start colouring your job yellow. If you don't like your job, imagine a new one that you will, and start looking for it. It only has to be one change better than where you are. Personally I'd like to play business like Richard Branson, but that isn't one step away for me, it's many, many, steps but I can take a step in that direction (I have my own little business and I support Kiva businesses).

Your happiness is worth moving jobs for.

If you're in a minimum wage, or zero hour contract job you hate, start by finding a minimum wage, or zero hour contract job that you love. There's more vacancies in low wage jobs than high paid ones. Take a stroll through the job ad pages and see what's out there. Why stick with a job you hate with poor pay, when there are places you'll be happier, which have the same wage? People get stuck in jobs they hate, frozen by the fear of change. Your happiness is worth moving jobs for.

Look at your sunshine clocks. If your nine to five is coloured grey, that's a large chunk of your life. Too much of your life. You deserve to be happy, so go create some happiness by finding a job where you are a good fit. You don't have to settle for a job where you don't fit. If you have chosen to go forth with positivity, find a business to work for, that has the same attitude.

I know that applying for loads of jobs is really hard, because I've had plenty of experience of it. However I've also been on loads of interview panels as a manager, and what that showed me is that it's unbelievably hard to recruit staff. It's hard to find engaged, positive people, who actually want to do the job you want them to do. If you get out of the job you hate, and identify where you want to work, and what kind of thing you want to do, you'll be one of these positive, happy people employers are looking for.

Unhappy people are well known for being very unproductive and bad for business. They drag everyone else down, and can sour a whole department. I was surprised to hear a friend admit that this was her in her previous job.

I think of her as a loving, giving person (and she is, in her current job), but obviously she wasn't being her true self in her previous job! (I can also remember not being the

If you can be happy to do
the job you're paid for,
you're hot property!

best fit in a couple of jobs I've had too). Sadly I also know someone who felt she had to close her shop, because she found out that customers were turning back at the door, when they saw particular staff serving on the counter. She told me it was just too hard to remove bad staff, and felt there were no good ones to recruit. She closed her shop and everyone lost their jobs.

What you may not have realised, is that if you can be happy to do the job you're paid for, you're hot property! Happy people motivate others to do the job well. Customers love them and want to interact with them. Happy people are really good for business. (Ever had a favourite barista?) In fact a young friend has just been promoted into management, because as well as being capable, her boss valued that she was always happy. A happy manager is a great motivator for a team, and a happy worker has a better chance of being promoted than an unhappy one.

So if you can find a business where you'll be happy, try asking for a job - don't wait for the adverts. Just get your foot in the door. So many businesses have jobs available that they never advertise. Interestingly Katie Fforde even wrote a short story about this for Quick Reads. 'Saving the Day' is an inspirational and motivational read, not to mention quick.

Think about place that you'd like to work.

1. *List* the kind of places where you fit.

2. *Think* about the kind of job where there will be people like you, whom you'll get on with. The atmosphere will be great. *Write* down single words, or your thoughts, and see where they lead you.

The most incredible and surprising work atmosphere I've ever experienced, was when I visited a hospice. The vibe was so loving and positive. It taught me to keep an open mind about different sectors.

3. *Write* down your interests here. Follow these, and see where they take you.

4. **Think** of any jobs you've had where things didn't work out? What can you learn about your interests and your fit?

I once had a shop floor job in a prestigious chain store, in the coveted department of 'ladies fashions'. Latest fashions really aren't my thing, and I grew to hate it because the supervisor clearly didn't like me. One time she told me I'd have to stand behind the till all day because of 'those things on your feet', which were just strappy sandals. Everyone else was wearing heeled shoes, but I didn't possess any of those. Another time she looked at my hands in disgust and told me to go and wash, ignoring my response that my finger cuticles were stained from coloured drawing inks and not dirty.

This woman really didn't seem to like having an art student in her team, and to be fair, although I really enjoyed helping the customers, I just didn't get excited by the latest rail of clothes coming in. Like I said, fashion really isn't my thing. I was definitely in the wrong place. A sensible boss would have redeployed me to another department, or behind the scenes, where I would have fitted better. Instead she continually made comments about how I looked, and crushed my self-esteem until I left. I was just a wrong fit.

Another time I heard that an Interior Designer was looking for someone for the workroom. The pay was lousy but the work looked fun. I turned up and asked to be given a trial. The boss was so passionate about his job that I liked being around him, and I liked being around his staff too. I got on well with them all. I was happy to do the job that was required, which was one that would never have been advertised.

In any kind of organisations or company, happiness flows from the top. Someone who is happy in their job, will enable you to be happy in yours. Look for an appreciative boss, who is a joy to work for. It makes all the difference. If you're that boss, practise some gratitude at the end of every shift by thanking your staff, and watch the happiness of your staff spiral up.

Are you still thankful? I am. It becomes a habit.

How's your Ship's Log coming along? How many bits a day are you colouring in now?

Get Out of Your Head Takeaway

Write here things that struck a chord with you that you want to remember or use for your Life Manual: (here are my prompts for you...)

- Beautiful, wonderful, thankful
- Favourite Oxytocin hits
- Sunshine clocks and yellow crayons
- My job

PAUSE
& REFLECT

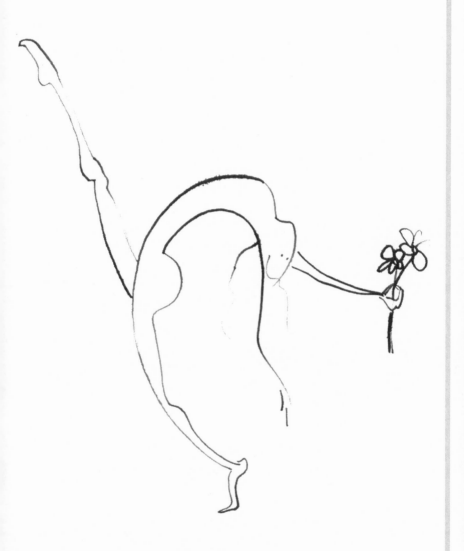

Chapter Four
Unleash Your Creativity

PAUSE
& REFLECT

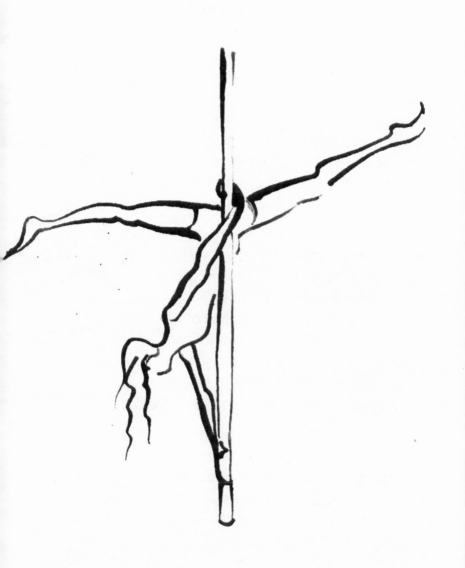

Try Something New

Try Something New

I believe just like the double helix of our DNA, we are travelling on a spiral through life. We need to keep our momentum going, spiralling upwards, to avoid spiralling downwards. Trying new things is a really good way to spiral upwards, because trying new things, getting out of your 'usual', will keep you moving upwards.

In the film *The Creative Brain*, Dr David Eagleman says that when you feel that there's something missing in your life, or if you are feeling depressed, the problem is caused by a lack of creativity. He says that the human race is meant to be creative and that trying new things enables us to harness our creativity, and therefore to live more creatively.

How this works is that when you start trying new things, you start making connections between disparate things. For instance, the scientist Michelle Khine revolutionised nanotechnology (tech working on the scale of atoms and molecules), by making an amazing link between her challenges at work, and Shrinky Dink toys from her childhood. Do you remember Shrinky Dinks? They were bits of special plastic, with drawings printed on them, that kids would colour in and then bake in the oven, to

The human race is meant to be creative.

make them shrink to a fraction of their size. As kids in the 70's, we then started doing the same thing with crisp packets, shrinking them to make keyring fobs. Michelle Khine realised that if she made normal sized technology (cheaper and easier than nanotechnology), and put it on the back of Shrinky Dink plastic, she could then heat up the whole thing, and it would all shrink to become teeny tiny nanotechnology. Clever eh? In that simple connection she revolutionised nanotechnology.

So that's two reasons for trying new things - to keep you spiralling upwards in life and to unleash your creativity.

The things that really work for you and help you spiral upwards, are still to be uncovered, or discovered, and that's where your Life Manual comes in. When you know what works for you, note it in the section at the end of this chapter including the recipe for it. The information is then all ready for a page of its own when you make your Life Manual. Once it's there, it's easy to be referred to when you need reminding.

Would you like to hear about my amazing 'new'? I've just tried oil painting because I visited a commercial art gallery, new to me. I fell in love with some paintings there by an artist, who was new to me, who paints in colours that make my soul sing. Curious about his painting materials, I then decided to find some answers by emailing this highly successful artist, new to me. He replied and expressed interest in my art and painting, new to me! So I showed him (someone outside my family) my drawings, new to me. Unlike other art professionals (past art teachers) he liked my drawings, new to me! Encouraged, I decided to book up on an oil painting lesson, new to me. The artist and I went on to start a correspondence all about painting, new to me. We seem to inspire each other to keep painting or drawing, new to me.

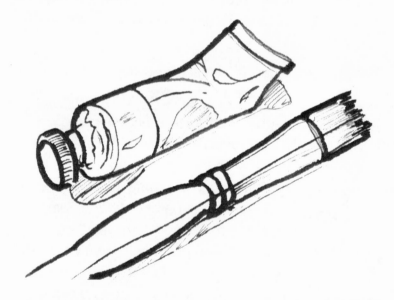

So trying something 'new to me', began very small, with something that caught my eye (an exhibition in a commercial art gallery) and has progressed, cascaded we could say, to me exhibiting paintings and publishing them in a book for all to see. Yep you guessed it, new to me.

Exercise:

1. *Choose* to try a 'new to me' today. It could be walking a different route to the shops, dancing to the radio, walking backwards to see a different view.

2. *Write* down five things that you could do in the next week, that are new to you.

3. *Write* in your Kindly Book, what you did and any chain reactions that began.

4. *Congratulate* yourself! You're doing really well.

How are your thankfuls going? Keep them up! Are you still using your Ship's Log or is your log simply becoming a way of life? Exciting isn't it.

PAUSE
& REFLECT

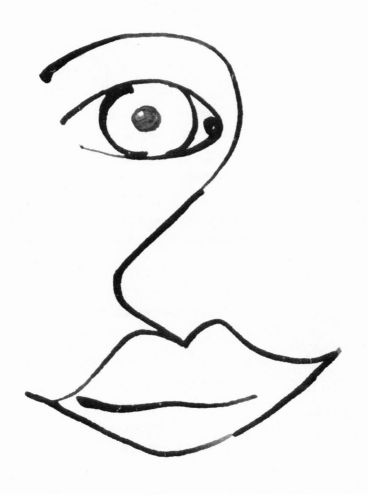

See Like An Artist

See Like An Artist

Now that I've started talking about creativity, there's no stopping me! This is a rather long chapter and if this book was published by someone other than my good self, this chapter would probably be severely cut. It is rather long. However here's the caveat from me. If you get bored, bale out and skip to the next chapter. It took me a long while to realise that when I give up on a non-fiction book I'm reading, it's because I've got from the book what I needed. So if that's you at any point in this chapter, then chop, chop, off you go (now there's an old fashioned phrase for you - no idea what was being chopped).

So here goes, read as much as you want and no more, but on your way past, have a look at the exercises at the end of the chapter.

Paradise: There is something special about the place your mind goes to when being creative. It's a beautiful, soothing, restful, other worldly place. A wonderful, easy place to be, which can also be really hard to get to. A bit like that wonderful paradise island, with clear waters and tropical palms, that isn't marked on the map and is hidden behind a shroud of

There is something special about the place your mind goes to when being creative.

fog, but with intention and persistence can be found.

It was interesting to note that when the first lockdown happened in 2020, and the whole country seemed to stop, there was a flurry of creativity from some artists, as if suddenly that paradise island was easier to access. A painter friend coyly admitted to enjoying the lockdown 'because I can paint all the time as we don't have visitors interrupting me'.

However, you don't have to be an accomplished or professional artist to enjoy creating art. The process itself is wonderful and therapeutic, and not dependent on the end product. The point is, to walk on that island in paradise, and anyone can do that.

The end product of art is so subjective, we really shouldn't ever be worrying about this. You only have to go and look at any art collection, to see a huge variation in what is valued as art.

If you had all the money in the world, would you really buy much of what is in famous art galleries? So never be your own critical art critic. Always be your own art patron instead.

The Van Gogh brother who says 'I like it, it's great, keep going'. This is what Theo Van Gogh said, even when the rest of the world ridiculed Vincent. Remember that no one else has to see your art, or like your art. Creating art, whether it's visual arts, 3D crafts, music, or dance, is your walk in paradise. Fuel for your soul.

You don't have to draw, or paint to be a visual artist. Most of being an artist, is about ways of seeing, and about your internal thoughts and feelings. If you'd like to, come be an artist with me:

Look at the world in front of you. The view before you is your picture frame.

Make a line drawing in your mind.

See the World as Lines:

Seek out the vertical lines.
Count each one you can see,
starting from the left, counting round to
the right hand side of your vision (you don't
have to actually count them, but it's a good
way of making you actually look at, and register each
one). I have to admit that when I try to count them, I lose
count pretty quick, that's just the way my brain works (or
doesn't!) but it's easy for me to look at each line along
its length, as if I were drawing it with a pencil, because
I've done a lot of holding a pencil. Notice the spaces
between the lines and how far apart they are. I'm sitting
in a canteen as I write this, and the pillars of the walls are
all becoming closer together as I look farther along the
wall on my left.

Next look for the horizontal lines in your picture frame,
count them again, just to make yourself actually look at
each one.

Next I look for any diagonal lines, and compare the
angle of the diagonal with either a horizontal line or a
vertical line. I can see the line where the wall meets the
ceiling. From where I'm sitting it's a diagonal.

If I were to hold my pen out at arm's length, with
a straight arm and pen held vertically, I could rotate
my pen like the hand of a clock, and align it with the
diagonal line I'm looking at. When my pen points at the
twelve (or six) on a clock face, these are true vertical
lines I can see. My pen pointing at the three (or nine)
of a clock, is the true horizontal lines I see. When I line

my pen up with the line that is the join between the wall and the ceiling, I can see that that line is like my pen pointing at the eleven (or five), of a clock. There are a row of large windows along the wall of the canteen, and when I rotate my outstretched pen to align with the bottom of the windows, my pen is pointing at a little before the nine of a clock. When I look at where the wall meets the floor, my pen is pointing between the 7 and 8 on a clock.

Now I'm looking for circles, or parts of circles, arcs. There aren't many here, I'm in a very geometric setting! I can only see the tops of the chair backs above the tables as arcs.

See the World in Technicolour:

Would you like to try a colour painting with me now? What colours can you see before you? If you can see a flat colour i.e. a red table or a grey building, look into the shadows. What are the colours you can see there? Are all shadows grey? Or have they some other colour?

If you're looking at something that is coloured black, how are shadows on the black different from the rest of the black? What about when something is white? What colour are the shadows on a white thing? Actually, is what you're calling white, really white? What is the difference between brilliant white ceiling paint, and the colour you're looking at? What colour would you have to add? Is the white 'borrowing' from the adjacent colour?

Has it taken on a blue hue, because it's next to a strong blue? Or have the artificial lights lent it some warm yellow (or worse, green!).

See the World in Lights and Darks:

Now you can do mind-drawing in line and in colour, do you want to try some other aspects? How about light and dark? Let's try monochrome painting. If you had just one colour, let's say blue, but you had all the shades of blue from a very light, white blue (a blue tint) all the way through to a very dark, black blue (a blue tone), how would you represent the scene in front of you?

What we're trying to do with this exercise is become aware of the lights and darks, and all the variations in between, without getting distracted by all the different colours. A bit like turning your full colour HD camera into an old fashioned black and white one. This exercise is a bit trickier, so choose a smaller picture frame than your whole vision before you, or choose just one object in front of you.

How about my coffee cup? The darkest bit is the coffee dregs in the cup, but there's also a tiny dark shadow where the cup meets the saucer. The lightest bits are little white spots in both the cup and saucer, reflecting the ceiling lights. The next lightest bits are significantly darker than these highlights, and are on the rim of the cup; the top surface of the handle, and the front rim of the saucer which is facing the window.

See the World in What's Not There:

Let's try perhaps the trickiest technique, negative spaces. Let's use a spindle backed chair as an example (can you tell I spend a lot of time in cafes?). The chair is constructed of wood, and has 5 wooden spindles set into the seat and supporting the top rail of the chair. If I look at the chair as negative spaces, I'm going to draw the air between the spindles, not the chair itself. The chair will appear as clean paper as I'm not interested in it. I'm interested in the spaces around the chair. The spaces between the spindles make rectangular picture frames. Within these I can see lines, shadows and colours. I can choose to 'draw' either the lines, shadows or colours, of the spaces, or all three.

When you're seeing like an artist, you're on your way to paradise.

Exercise:

1. **Look** up from this page, what do you see? Do a quick line drawing in your head.

2. **Start** a line drawing in your head, next time you are paused somewhere, whether in a supermarket queue, or a traffic jam, or somewhere altogether more inspiring.

3. **Try** a colour study in your head. Today I was looking at the exact blue of the sky and noticing the exact grey hues of the floating clouds.

4. **Look** into shadows and spot the colours, next time you're somewhere grey and uninspiring. There will be some colours hiding, waiting to be discovered by you.

Colour in the palette on your Ship's Log every time you've thought like an artist, even if you only had one fleeting thought - that's a good start!

How's the Ship's Log going? Can you see your progress? Be proud of yourself! I'm sending love and feeling proud of you! Are you still thankful? There's more to be thankful for than you ever thought, isn't there?!

When you're seeing like
an artist, you're on your way to paradise.

PAUSE
& REFLECT

Design Your Own Beauty Spot

Design Your Own Beauty Spot

I hope you survived the last chapter. Did you have fun as an artist? Did you discover paradise?

Have you ever seen Yoga by Adrienne on the internet? When I look at Adriene's videos, I see a beautiful, serene woman in a beautiful serene apartment, and I think 'I'd love to live there'. I however, bought a house listed as 'a project', and I moved in with an on-going project of a baby gestation. The two were always mutually exclusive. Despite a never-ending renovation project though, I can still have a beautiful home - well part of a home. For me it may sometimes be limited to a bunch of supermarket flowers in a jug, but it's a beauty spot never the less. Let's call it a bijou beauty spot (with soft focus on all the surrounding family and DIY debris).

Sometimes we can be so overwhelmed by life that it's hard to know where to start to make changes, so we don't. We just chase our tails in overwhelm. For me there was so much to do in the house, that the sensible solution would have been to gut every room, and start from scratch. But how could I gut a house and live there at the same time? How can we do big projects, when we have so many other demands on our time, and all our time is broken into little fragments?

After a while I didn't even notice the tattiness, all the bits that didn't have that light, airy, minimalist look. However, even when we're not conscious of it, clutter has a way of encroaching on our soul. There's something not good about clutter that we absorb, or maybe it's the flip; there's something good for our souls that the clutter stops us from absorbing?

Well-meaning friends would advise me on what I should do first, usually something practical, or something in desperate need. Others would help to make a significant difference, but I found that it was only when a candle of joy was lit in one place, that the light spread outwards and my home really started to transform.

So I recommend a counter intuitive renovation. Make one small place a place of beauty. Be it a shelf with an ornament, or a chair with an inviting cushion, or a corner with a plant, and then watch the beauty spread out from that corner. Jealously guard that beautiful space to stop the tide of clutter encroaching on it, keep sweeping it back! Retain the beauty. That little patch of beauty, will teach you to seek beauty. It will spark joy. It will reach out its light a bit further, and a little bit more further, until a whole corner looks beautiful, then a whole room. Harness beauty to do the work for you. You will find it spreads.

I started by buying myself a bunch of flowers to stand in a vase, and look beautiful for me. I chose the smallest cheapest bunch, from the cheapest supermarket. However these flowers brought me such joy and delight, made such a difference to my time at home, that I was suddenly awakened to my cluttered existence, and decided to create more joy.

I chose as my starting place, a place that really bugged me, a place filled with ghosts, and sucked the life from my soul every time I saw it. This sounds rather dramatic and exaggerated, but it was a small part of my house that was a constant reminder of my broken dreams. A place where a painting that symbolised my life's dreams used to hang, before those dreams were shattered. This was not the place that any outside, objective person would have started because the decor was actually in reasonable condition. However, if I had been asked to make a list of the places in my home that made me feel the worst, this would have been it. I needed to exorcise this wall, and reclaim it as beautiful to me.

As I was feeling skint, I used a pot of bright turquoise paint (a colour that fills me with joy), left over from painting a bedroom wall, to paint my living room wall with. I then emptied old picture frames and refilled them with artwork that I found beautiful and inspiring, which in my case was artwork by my family. Et voila!

My own personal art gallery.
This shone a light out into the
room. Suddenly the shelves
in the alcove next to the new
gallery looked messy and ugly, so
I was motivated to clear the storage
stuff off them, and use them instead as
display shelves for some beautiful (to me!) objects
that I had hidden away. Then I decided I wanted to
highlight my display, so I painted the wall behind the
shelves with some grey paint I had. And so it went on,
the beauty spread outwards. At every stage I felt joy
and energy. Quite different from the usual overwhelm. I
loved the colours I was working with, I loved the objects
I was wanting to display. I was no longer trudging and
begrudging a chore I had to do. I was enjoying myself.
The wind of change was whistling pleasantly around me.

My little foray into the land of beauty and colour
continued. Some good luck followed in the form of
a friend who, so impressed by the transformation I'd
achieved, offered to paint my ceiling for me. The result
was so transformational he asked to paint the remaining
walls, and did a far better job that I ever would, because
he filled and sanded all the little holes left from decades
of picture hooks. Wow the result
was amazing! By now the room was
definitely on its way up!

So you see, what all started
out with me buying a cheap
bunch of flowers for myself at a
supermarket, spiralled upwards

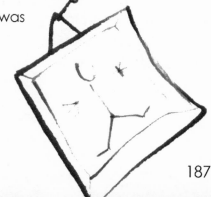

Make one small place a place of beauty.

and I ended up with a beautiful, tranquil room. The beauty spread outwards and my energy levels soared upwards. I attracted good luck; the hardest bit (painting the ceiling), was done by someone else as a gift. In a physical sense, this maintained my energy levels because I didn't have to do it, and in a spiritual sense, it boosted my energy levels because I felt so excited, joyful and grateful. Who could have known that a little bunch of flowers could achieve so much?

Exercise:

1. **Think** of one easily achievable thing you could do to transform a part of your home you hate, into a beauty spot. **Write** it here.

It could be as simple as putting some flowers in a vase, or clearing the clutter off a beautiful piece of furniture to reveal its glory, or throwing out mismatched pillow cases and buying a matching set, or binning the tatty old tea towels and replacing them with the 'for best' ones you keep in your drawer, or cleaning a window to look all sparkly and bright.

2. **Do** this thing. Give yourself a big tick and smily emoji, here, when you've done it.

3. **List** ten tiny things that you could do to make your home more beautiful. It could be clean one window, hang one picture, put your favourite duvet cover on your bed.

1.   6.

2.   7.

3.   8.

4.   9.

5.   10.

4. **Bookmark** this page. Over the next few weeks, start doing your ten tiny things. Challenge yourself to finish them. Put a line through each item when you do it and write the completion date next to it.

Every time you make something beautiful, even if it's only removing the clutter that's accumulated since you cleared the top of your favourite bit of furniture, **colour** in the flower on your Ship's Log. Can you see how far you've come? Keep sailing with me. It's worth it. You're worth it. And I'm thankful you're coming on this journey with me. What are you thankful for?

Unleash Your Creativity Takeaway

Write here things that struck a chord with you, that you want to remember or use in your Life Manual: (here are some prompts...)

- Try something new.
- See like an artist.
- Design your own beauty spot.

PAUSE
& REFLECT

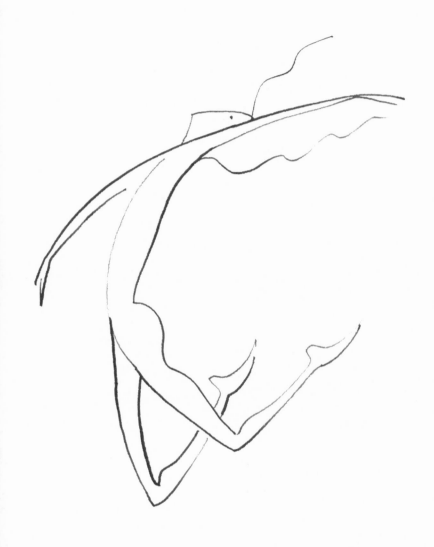

Chapter Five
You Are Wonderful

PAUSE
& REFLECT

For Every Wart There's A Wow

For Every Wart There's A Wow

I'm hoping by now that there is some beauty in your life. Maybe a bunch of flowers in a jug, a beautiful greetings card you've bought for yourself and put on your mantelpiece, or perhaps you've started using some of the bed linen or towels you've been keeping for best? I'm so glad that beauty is swirling into your life, for you are a human being, and you are wonderful. Did you know that? The design of the human being is amazing. If you thought of yourself as a spirit that chose to occupy a human body, wouldn't you agree that the human is amazing?

If you were handed the true person specification for being the true you, who you really are, you would be wowed. Believe me. You would be. You would instantly realise your worth as a person. You would realise that you are fantastic. None of us are born with this knowledge. If we are lucky, we discover it bit by bit. However if you look for your wonderfuls, you'll be wowed.

If you look for your wonderfuls, you'll be wowed.

We are all wonderful human beings, but the combination of humans that we relate to throughout our lives, sometimes mean this knowledge doesn't flourish.

The philosopher Alain De Botton is fascinated by our relationships with each other. He's also fascinated by our oddities, and how they affect our relationships. He says that our

You're a very special person,
just needing the right kind
of air to thrive.

oddities may take us a lifetime to discover, however our friends know what they are, within ten minutes of our first acquaintance. I talk of wonderful attributes. He talks of oddities. How useful though, would it be if we had some awareness of our wonderfulness, our oddities, and our deviations from the norm? If we knew our attributes, finding a job that we excel at, which satisfies us, would be so much easier. In new relationships, we could exchange key information with our partners 'This is how I'm odd' and from that hopefully, we could have more tolerance of, and understanding for, each other. We could help each other uncover the wonderful person they really are.

My son recently told me that I have 'silly-voice Tourette's'. Rubbish I thought. Not long afterwards I was saying an emotional farewell to a much loved visitor. "Goodbye" I squeaked in a Mickey Mouse voice. I tried again but only proved my son right. My whole life uncoiled behind me like a ball of string. My cheeks flushed pink. How could I not have ever known this? He's right, I do have silly-voice Tourettes!

Doesn't it make so much sense, that if we had an understanding of our talents and oddities, we would find life and seeking rewarding paid work, easier? I guess this is what Ms Myers and Ms Brigg thought when they designed the Myers Brigg test in the 1960s, which is still used by businesses today. They define sixteen different types, all based on the way you process your thinking. There is no one type that is better than the other, but there are types that are far more common, or far more rare. One type in fact is estimated to be only 1.5% of the population. So if you feel that there's nobody quite like you, in the case of the INFJ type, you are almost right. I decided to take the free version of the test online.

www.truity.com/test/type-finder-personality-test-new

The question answering format was a scale of 'strongly agree' to 'strongly disagree'. I was rather non-plussed, as I noncommittally plumped for middle ground after middle ground, in what seemed like endless questions, but as I got through this muddy middle, the pace hotted up and I found it much easier producing answers way up at either end of the scale. Then out popped my complex profile of four simple letters.

My results appeared and I was able to read the lowdown of what I am like. A bit like reading about my birth sign, but far more accurate. The first few of my declared attributes, I could have easily guessed without being told, but then the surprises arrived: It turns out that all my oddities and inconsistencies of character are entirely predictable and a feature of my 'type' (although admittedly not the silly-voice Tourette's). In the list of suitable jobs, I was able to tick off 50% I'd already done. Next came the compatibility chart for relationships, and

Let's stick with focusing on the wows.

a block of basically no-go relationships (although from experience, I wouldn't say it was exhaustive...).

What I conclude from this is that firstly I wish I'd had the no-go relationships list at age 20, so I knew who to avoid. And secondly I can stop beating myself up about some dumb life decisions I've made, because a) my character is pre-programmed for dumb decisions and b) I am pre-programmed to beat myself up about dumb decisions. The overall result is that I now find I'm much kinder to myself because I can totally accept how I am, warts and all. It is just me, and to put it another way, for every wart there's a wow.

What wows do you have, where you might have seen warts? If you're forgetful, are you also very good at being adaptable? If you're rather anxious, does this make you a very thorough planner? If you're a fidget, does this mean you're very good at sports? If you're a daydreamer, are you a good creator? If you're 'too chatty', does this make you great at customer facing jobs?

Let's make a pact. Let's all stick with focusing on the wows. Let's celebrate our wows together.

Exercise:

1. **List** five 'warts' that you think you have

   1.

   2.

   3.

   4.

   5.

2. **Look** at your list and start flipping those warts. For every wart you should be able to find at least one wow.

   1.

   2.

   3.

   4.

   5.

Thank goodness
there's you in the world.

3. **Write** down five more wows. A new line for each. Add some decoration. Thank goodness there's you in the world.

1.

2.

3.

4.

5.

How are your thankfuls today? Perhaps tomorrow your wows will be in your list?

When you realise you have a wow, **colour** the wow in on your Ship's Log. This is quite a hard one to achieve, unless you're practised at flipping: Every time you catch yourself thinking something negative about yourself, or every time you find what you think is a wart, flip it and find the wow. Colour in the wow in your Ship's Log whenever you do this and be proud of yourself. You're a very special person, just needing the right kind of air to thrive.

PAUSE
& REFLECT

Twelve Birthdays

Twelve Birthdays

So now you know how wonderful you are, let's really start celebrating! In our busy lives it can be hard to find the time for fun, and that's where scheduling in fun time is a good strategy, and what better way to remember to have fun, than to indulge yourself every month on the anniversary of date when you were born? You can have twelve birthdays, and you don't even have to age! Mark this down in your diary or on your calendar so you remember to do something special to treat yourself.

Your celebrations needn't be hard to achieve. For instance, on my twelfth birthday this month, I'm going to sit down and watch a whole film that is just for me. Not to learn anything, not to accommodate a family member's age, or choices. Just for me. I'll also choose a treat of my choice to indulge in. I think a cake for one would be nice.

Plan out the whole day to be special. Enjoy the preparations. What clothes do you love to wear, that bring you joy? Were you keeping them for best? Get these out ready. Is there a place or activity that would help you to air your happy clothes? Do you need to arrange an evening date with a friend to give you a reason and venue to dress up? To wear the beautiful but impractical shoes?

Or if wearing a wetsuit is more your style, do you need to arrange a beach swim, or some water sports?

Is there a meal you really love? Every yearly birthday in our house the celebrant has the honour of designing the menu (based on the cook's - or supermarket's - abilities) and this involves a lot of anticipation, decisions and great excitement. A lot of the fun of a celebration is the build up, so remember to revel in this part too.

What would you really like to do. What things would you love to do in the next five years, which could be achieved in less than a day each?

Share these with your friends. Tell them about twelfth birthdays. Perhaps they could help make your dreams come true? Or you could use your connections to make their dreams come true? This is how my friend's bucket list on Facebook worked. She'd always wanted to go up in a light aircraft, and a pilot friend of a friend, of a friend, offered to take her up. But let's not wait for a terminal diagnosis. Let's live our lives to the full anyway. Some things might be ambitious and need planning, but there are plenty to find that won't. What will you do first?

I wonder how many of your dreams

could be achieved if you reached out and made them visible?

Biographers have discovered that all the artists who've 'made it', did so because not only did they have talent, but they also reached out and formed networks with relevant others (artists and galleries and publishers etc), and this made their art visible. So want a ride in a flash car, or on the back of a fast motorcycle? Ask the next driver you see. Want to groom a horse? Turn up at a stable yard and ask if you can help. Want to go to a comedy show? Tell all your friends. Make your dreams visible.

In the film, *The Pursuit of Happyness* which is based on a true story, Will Smith's character, Gardner, approaches a well dressed man getting out of a red Ferrari. Gardner is so in awe of the car he asks the owner "What do you do?" (the real Gardner really did this). What happened next is a piece of pure magic; the Ferrari driver agrees to meet up with Gardner and explain to him the basics of Wall Street. This sets Gardner on a path to incredible riches, which without the Ferrari drivers help, he wouldn't have been able to achieve.

I love this story because it demonstrates how you don't

I wonder how many of your dreams could be achieved if you reached out and made them visible?

have to have the whole thing figured out. You just have
to take a small step in the right direction. Every time I read
about a person who's 'made it big', it always turns out
they got a 'lucky break' somewhere along the way. You
never know when yours will turn up, but you have to be
on that path.

Exercise 1:

1. *List* 12 things you love to do that could be achieved
tomorrow (eat lemon cheese cake, wear my best
matching lingerie set)

   1.

   2.

   3.

   4.

   5.

   6.

   7.

   8.

   9.

   10.

   11.

   12.

2. *List* 12 things you'd love to do in the next five years that would take a bit of plannning (ride pillion on a big motorbike, go skinny dipping, walk on a beach at night, toast marshmallows over a fire, go to a comedy club). This is what intentional living is.

1.	7.
2.	8.
3.	9.
4.	10.
5.	11.
6.	12.

3. *Mark* on your calendar every twelfth birthday

4. *Plan* the details of your next twelfth birthday.

5. *Celebrate* your twelfth birthday!

Now you know how good it feels, learn even more about how to have good times:

Exercise 2:

Every twelfth birthday...

1. **Write** a special entry, a review, in your Kindly Book entitled 'Celebrating me'. Try it now.

2. **List** all the bestest good things that have happened to you in the past month. Write at least 5 things.

3. **Ask** yourself 'why did they happen?' and write down the answers. As you find the answers, you will find a strategy appearing. Your unconscious, can then move to your conscious.

On your Ship's Log, every time you celebrate your twelfth birthday, **colour** in your birthday candle and make a wish out loud!

What were your thankfuls today? What did you draw on your Ship's Log today? Look at your Ship's Log: How has your passage been? I'm sure you've covered some distance. That was fine sailing ship mate! It's been a privilege to sail with you.

You Are Wonderful Takeaways

Write here things that struck a chord with you that you want to remember or use for your Life Manual. Did you find any strategies appearing for having good times? (here are my prompts for you):

- My warts and wows.
- My twelve birthdays.

PAUSE
& REFLECT

Chapter Six
The Future Looks Bright

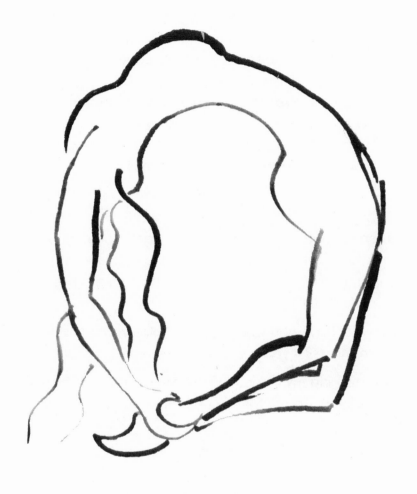

The End Is Just The Beginning

The End Is Just The Beginning

As we're nearing the end of this part of how To Love & Be Loved, I want you to join with me in imagining a different future. One that's already in existence, but has further still to grow. This whole book has been about loving life, loving your life. Even loving you. When you love life, life loves you back. That's how it works. Like attracts like. Have you felt my love for you? You picked up this book. It's in your hands and within it, is love from my heart.

This book is just the start of what I want to say. As soon as it is published, I'll be editing Part Two. It's already written, but was too big for just one book. You need a break to let the sediment settle before I start making more ripples, but before I go, I want to give you a glimpse of the world that I've seen.

How far have you sailed with me? Are you still writing your thankfuls? If you are you'll have seen it too...

Keep sailing my friend. You are the captain of your own Ship. Set your course for fairer weather. You can see the way.

PAUSE
& REFLECT

A Kinder Business

A Kinder Business

I've spent years working with, or in, or starting social enterprises, - enterprises created for the social good they do - and so my ear is tuned for hearing great stories.

When we put love at the top of the list, the world changes. It's radical but simple. For example there are businesses, (both private and not-for-profits) that reside in love, that do business very gently, including valuing the welfare of their employees above profit. Interestingly it turns out this approach is also pretty good for business finances.

Can I tell you another story? I heard of an American manufacturer, who when the financial crash hit in 2008, decided not to make redundancies, because that would transfer the financial hardship to the lives of those who could least absorb it. So instead the boss told the entire workforce that at some point over the next year, every single employee would have to take four weeks unpaid leave, because the company needed to save $10million. However, he also said that they could take the unpaid leave at any time, and it didn't have to be all in one chunk. That was twenty days unpaid leave. It could be half a day off a week. It could be four weeks in a row. Everyone would lose one-thirteenth of their annual salary. This was how the company would save the money they needed to.

When we put love at the top of the list, the world changes.

So unlike many other businesses, everyone there kept their jobs. However an unforeseen thing happened; staff began trading their unpaid time off between themselves so that those who could afford the pay cut, took an even bigger pay cut, and more time off, helping those who could least afford the pay cut, to avoid it. That company survived the downturn. I can only guess at the goodwill and loyalty the staff felt to the company for this kindness.

I remember the impact on my family when my dad's employer went bust and my dad was out of work for fifteen months. The family relationships changed over night. This period in my life proved pivotal to my attitudes as an adult towards money and employment. The consequences were far reaching. As a parent now myself, I know the effect that big stresses have on parenting. The personal distress avoided by that company's decision not to make redundancies, cannot be measured. But it can be felt, can't it? I can feel it even now. What if everyone put love first?

Sharing the problems openly with your staff, resonates with the research done by the academic Alex Soojung-Kim Pang. His research shows that when open and honestly consulted and empowered, employees have contributed to the efficient running of a businesses in ways that could not have been predicted. He discovered that shorter working weeks could actually increase a company's profits. The key was employee involvement matched with employee benefit. When employees understood the big picture and were given the scope to improve their own time management, in return for some kind of personal gain (like extra time off), amazing things happened. Businesses not only found they did the same job quicker, but they had better staff retention and their profits soared.

This finding also tallies with the story I heard of the sales person who decided to vary her own work hours to suit herself. She realised that if she stayed in the office for an hour after it closed at 9pm, she could pick up all the customer calls that would normally go to answerphone, and easily meet her daily sales target in just that one hour. This was an amazing efficiency saving from a creative thinking employee!

These stories all prove that love, kindness and compassion are no threat to business profits. The more we share the good news stories of how kindness is good for the world, the quicker kindness will spread. In fact I shared the first story above, with a business owner who had a bit of a cashflow crisis after expanding. Others had been telling her she needed to immediately make staff redundant. I told her about the $10,000,000 budget cut story. What she actually did in the end, was sat down with her whole team and shared her problems. The result of this was that one employee volunteered to reduce her hours, because she wanted to spend more time with her young kids. The other employees accepted reducing their hours immediately, but offered ideas to the boss and jointly worked out a plan with her, for pulling the business through the sticky patch. I think it's good to share these stories. Kindness needs more visibility. We need more role models.

What could you do to raise the visibility of kindness? Perhaps we can share more stories?

I hope you will join me in listening out for, and collecting these stories, even if only to give yourself evidence that a revolution is quietly beginning. Perhaps you could even share these stories with me? Perhaps I should be writing them all down in a new book? Who knows what could happen when we all start thinking about it together?

Share with me: **stories@thecompanyofsmiles.co.uk**

Kindness needs more visibility. We need more role models.

PAUSE
& REFLECT

Gentle by Design

Gentle by Design

The thing about love is that it changes everything, in multiple tiny ways, but creating big effects, because it works as a cascade. Remember the cascade effect in Yellowstone Park? Well as I said at the beginning of this book, the people who introduced the wolves there, never predicted the impact the wolves would have on the course of the river. It was a cascade effect they started; they introduced wolves, which made the deer timid, which preserved the willow trees, which enabled the beavers to build dams, which made the river slow and meander. Hey Presto! Cascade! When we act in love and start a cascade of love, we can never know the full or final effect of that single drop of love, but it will be bigger and further reaching than we can ever imagine.

If we loved life, would we love all of life? Would we love every living thing? People and plants? Animals and insects? Fish and forests? If we loved all these, in what way would our world look different? Perhaps we'd create projects that facilitated human interaction and support, that were environmentally friendly and sustainable, that embraced the natural world, that shared resources between all?

We can never
know the full effect of a
single drop of love, but it will be bigger
and further reaching than we can ever imagine.

When we focus on love, things begin to look different. Take a project I've been working on recently. A community organisation concerned about high rents for homes in the UK, has negotiated with their council to buy a disused Care (Nursing) Home from them, to convert into flats, and provide low cost accommodation for local people. Their council is prioritising love for people over profit. The group's priority is to design the new flats for the maximum benefit of the new residents, as opposed to designing for maximum profit, as a commercial company would.

As there is a lack in their city of accommodation for single people, a conversion to one bedroom flats seemed the way to go. Loving all people, they decided that all the ground floor flats should be accessible for anyone with mobility issues, just in case. To accommodate the increasing longing for connectedness and support from fellow human beings (which increased greatly through the pandemic), they decided to develop the site using co-housing principles (www.co-housing.org.uk): the site would be intentionally designed to create opportunities for human interactions.

There would be a mixture of private and communal spaces, residents would share a meal once a week in the communal kitchen-diner, other shared facilities would be created as desired. The group believe that tenants should feel that they have some control over their lives, so they decided to immediately form a group of prospective tenants and get them involved in the design and the development of the flats. A grant enabled expert help to transform the group of individuals looking for homes, into a strong co-operative enterprise, so that the members would feel control, connectedness and mutual support straight away. A cascade of love began.

An architect drew up plans for the building's refurbishment. These drawings were shared at public meetings, so that the surrounding community, as well as the fledgling co-op, could have an input into the designs. As a result of this, it was decided to preserve the original Care Home's laundry, so that each flat didn't need the space, nor the budget for individual washing machines, and residents would be spared the inconvenience of using a public laundrette.

I don't know about you, but I have vivid memories of the hassle of laundrette trips, stuffing my rucksack with dirty laundry and trudging to the laundrette with my carefully saved coins, only to find I'd forgotten my soap powder and the soap dispenser at the laundrette wasn't working (as I type this I'm suddenly remembering a certain ad for Levi's jeans which is far more pleasant, which boosted the sales of boxer shorts

When we act in
love we start a cascade.

as well as jeans in UK...). Having your own personal laundrette sounds like another way of creating human connections and making laundry fun.

The invitation for ideas also resulted in a surprise change to the layout: Some of the younger members of the new co-op liked the idea of flat-sharing, so some of the proposed flats were combined and re-drawn to make a larger flat-share, making the housing even more affordable (government guidelines indicate rent of a room is about 65% of the rent of a one bed flat). The group also identified that in order to have a mixed, intergenerational community, they wanted some two bed flats and even one three-bed flat, which could accommodate a larger or older family group. The kindness continued as when the council was told of the plans to make some of the flats accessible for people with mobility issues, they linked the architect with their Occupational Therapist, for some expert input around the needs of people with mobility issues. A rather unique partnership.

The cascade continued. The energy and enthusiasm of the fledgling co-op group grew as the project evolved, and they started looking for a project of their own. Following on from all the thinking about the outside area, and how it could incorporate a shared growing space, the group decided to approached the local primary school and offer to run a gardening club for the local children. So a small community group looking to solve local housing issues, initiated a cascade which resulted in school children learning vegetable growing. Something nobody could have foreseen, and it's still early days. Who knows where the project will go next?

Another example of a cascade of love is the documentary film 'The Biggest Little Farm' in which a couple of Los Angeles city dwellers, with a love for nature, raise money from friends to buy a redundant, dry, arid, lemon farm. To work with nature, they are advised to begin by bringing microscopic life back into the soil. Their comittment to farming worms, to create worm pee, to revitalise the soil with microbes, started a cascade effect which ultimately produced a lush, diverse and highly productive farm. When the Los Angeles fires raged across the dry parched land of neighbouring farms, the Biggest Little Farm is miraculously saved, because their method of farming in harmony with nature, created a unique weather system over the farm, which held the fires at bay. The worms and microbes they introduced to their soil ultimately saved their farm from burning up the same way their neighbour's farms had. Just like the wolves who changed the river, the worms saved the farm from fires. We can never predict the ultimate effects of these cascades.

Think of all the jobs you've ever done. How would they change if love was the guiding principle? How would you redesign those jobs using love?

I was in a friend's terraced house today. The day was warm and beautiful, but the house was chilly and dark. I was looking at her little plot of land and thinking where her house would have been positioned in the plot, if it had been designed to embrace the light and warmth of the sun, instead of following the line of the road. How would a house look if it was part of the natural world, rather than just the manmade world?

About twenty years ago I visited another friend's house, which was designed by an eco-architect. Kate had bought a walled garden, sold off as a building plot. Rather unusually, instead of building the house slap in the middle of the plot as is the norm, she built the house right up against the northern boundary, with big south-facing windows looking out over the garden. The house was wonderfully light and inspiring.

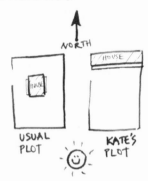

For years after, I dreamed of finding a house where I could build a south facing extension (I couldn't afford a plot and newbuild), to overlook the garden. Eventually I found a small east/west facing farm cottage with a big garden along one side, facing south. Bingo! I designed an extension with an open plan kitchen-diner, with patio doors overlooking the side garden to maximise the natural light and warmth. Three years ago the extension eventually got built. The design began a cascade effect: The room is always light and airy, lifting my mood. When I watch the changing weather and seasons it connects me with nature and seems to sooth my soul. Seeing the sky encourages me to go get some Sky On My Head, which always enhances my wellbeing. If the rest of the cottage didn't exist, I wouldn't care because the new room is so lovely, I'm rarely anywhere else.

Feeling the warmth of the sun through the large windows makes me very aware of the daily weather, and on cool days, very grateful for the warmth the sun brings. On hot days, the sun's warmth coming through the large windows is absorbed in the solid floor. This not only keeps the room from overheating, but it produces warm evenings too, as the heat is slowly released back out like a storage heater, so even after the sun has gone down, I'm still appreciating the wonder of its warmth under my feet.

Gratitude keeps me upbeat and as electricity prices start to soar, I'm grateful that I rarely need the lights on. When the wind blows, I'm grateful for the waving willows. When the rain flows, I'm grateful that I'm inside and dry. When the sun breaks through the clouds, I'm grateful to notice it. When the seasons change, I'm grateful for their continuous cycle. The desire to welcome the sun and the sky in seems to have created a cascade of love in my heart.

Can you think of any examples where love has been designed in?

Pause, breathe, have faith in love, and see where the flow takes us.

The most obvious example is a hospice, where the love is tangible as you step through the door. But what about designs by engineers, loving the gifts of the natural world and designing ways of working with the energy of the wind and sun, and hopefully minimising our impact on the earth?

There is so much abundance in the natural world: Like I began by saying, if we eat all the apples from a tree this year, next year more will grow, without us building a new tree, paying the tree or telling it what to do. It grows because it's alive and part of life. But if we fail to recognise this amazing fact, and chop the tree down, and kill it, we deprive ourselves of this gift. The natural world is an amazing, self-sustaining world. Working against it is like paddling upstream, when we could be using the current, and going with the flow. Going with the flow is far easier. We don't have to sacrifice a good life, we can actually find a better life. We can just pause in what we're doing. Pause, breathe, have faith in love, and see where the flow takes us.

Life and love is all around us. We can make teeny tiny adjustments to choose to live our lives in love, loving all living things. When we feel a connection, new choices and solutions appear, wholistic and collaborative solutions, like the Occupational Therapist talking to the architect. Teeny tiny adjustments.

Think of five teeny tiny actions from the last month that you took for love? Write them in the hearts below.

Maybe you stashed a shopping bag in your handbag/ rucksack so you won't get caught out again and have to buy more plastic? Maybe you paused a bit longer to talk to your elderly neighbour when taking the bins out so their day was brightened? Maybe you admired the weather and hung your washing out and got some Sky On Your Head rather than using the tumbledryer, saving electricity? Maybe you sat in a shopping centre, seeing like an artist instead of shopping like a celebrity, so reducing your consumption? If you can think of even one thing, congratulate yourself. Celebrate your conscious changes. What about five new teeny tiny actions for love you could try?

Write down teeny tiny actions for love, which you could take in the next month.

Maybe you could try walking to a place instead of driving? Inviting a friend to share some food instead of eating alone? Phoning your friend instead of texting? Buy an oat milk latte instead of a cows milk one (less cow flatulence equals more ozone layer)? What changes could your try? Congratulate yourself for every one. We need to celebrate more. We need to celebrate our teeny tinies. Draw your own heart, with your own name on it, in the space over the page, because I think you are a beautifully designed human and the future looks bright.

How's your Ship's Log going?

Connections

Connections

All through this book I've been talking about connecting. Connecting with life, with fellow humans, with nature, with creativity, with joy, with love. Connection is love. If you've got this far, I've connected with you.

Before I leave you, I'd like you to think of your five preferred ways for connecting with other people. Do you like meeting for coffee and cake? Walking in a park? Running around a park? Playing some music? Listening to music? Meeting with people who have the same interests as you? Discussing a book?

Who could join you in these things?

Make a list of people you'd like to connect with, matched up with activities.

People: **Activities:**

What about if you were really bold and brave? Who would you connect with then? What if you were brave for just two minutes, what could you do to connect with someone new? Could you say hello to someone you often see when you're on your usual travels? Could you give someone a compliment (everyone likes to receive them) to connect with them? Could you carry something with you that is a conversation piece for your hobby? I used to ride a box bike, transporting my kids around. A really unusual looking bike, I had so many conversations around it! Dog lovers walk about with their dog, which creates an opening for a conversation. Perhaps you have a bag or a brooch you've made?

Perhaps you could wear something that could be a conversation piece to help others connect with you? I had a conversation with someone in a carpark the other day, just because their T-shirt said something like 'Excuse me if all I talk about is cars, I'm a car-nut' so I commented on their odd little car and told them about my dad's bubble car. I think the conversation brightened both of our days, because he waved at me the next day when driving past.

How about, when it's your birthday, wear a big badge proclaiming this. Just think how many smiles you'd collect? Or instead of waiting, wear it on your 1/12 birthday and explain the concept?

Write below any things you can think of for your conversation piece.

Could you walk into a local club of people with your interest, knowing you can hide behind the activity you'll be doing?

Could you go to a market and chat to an un-busy stallholder? As owner-operators, they're usually passionate about what they do, and are keen to chat to pass the time and keep boredom at bay, so you're doing them a favour.

Could you post ads around your locality saying 'I like books (or knitting or baking etc) and I'll be at the cafe every Tuesday at 11am hoping to chat about shared interests'. Take along a book or something to keep you company. Remember everything is a matter of perspective: If you expect to simply have a nice cuppa every week, you won't be disappointed, and if someone turns up to join you, it's a bonus!

Think of five real life situations you know, where if you were brave for two minutes you could connect with someone new. **Write** them below:

Next step is in your own time, have a go at connecting. I'll be there alongside you. Cheering you on.

The Future Looks Bright
Takeaways

Write down here any notes for yourself. Maybe you've remembered some new things for your Life Manual. Maybe you're ready to schedule a manual-making day?

PAUSE
& REFLECT

Chapter Seven
Getting It Together

PAUSE
& REFLECT

A Peek Inside My Manual

A Peek Inside My Manual

As I put the finishing touches to my manuscript, correct the typos and remove the apostrophes I've erroneously scattered, as liberally as grounds of black pepper, as I struggle to learn the intricacies of metadata and kindle uploads, as I try to squash Indigo into a scanner and map her to a vector (isn't that a kind of dinosaur?) or turn her tiffs into gifs, as covid at last seems to be subsiding into a virus we can cope with, as I feel I'm really starting to get my stuff together, there's news of another catastrophe and I have to reach for my manual again.

I will stand up tall and hug the world. I will shut my eyes and take deep breaths. I will send feelings of love to the world.

Then as my manual tells me, I will pick up my paintbrush to go out of my mind and into the beauty and colours of my paints. When nobody's home I will blast out George Ezra and dance around my kitchen with the abandonment of a pre-schooler. I will scrawl the flowers Indigo wants to hold and splodge them with watercolours. I will tip my face to feel the warmth of the sun and admire the beauty of plants. I will walk down the beach and paddle in the waves. I will search for sea glass. I will go to the pool and put myself through my 1km paces. I will plan a movie night with my kids. I will invite a friend for tea. I will zoom with my childhood friends and ask for book recommendations. I will seek out some podcasts. I will go collecting my hugs.

And that's just what I need. What about you? What do you need?

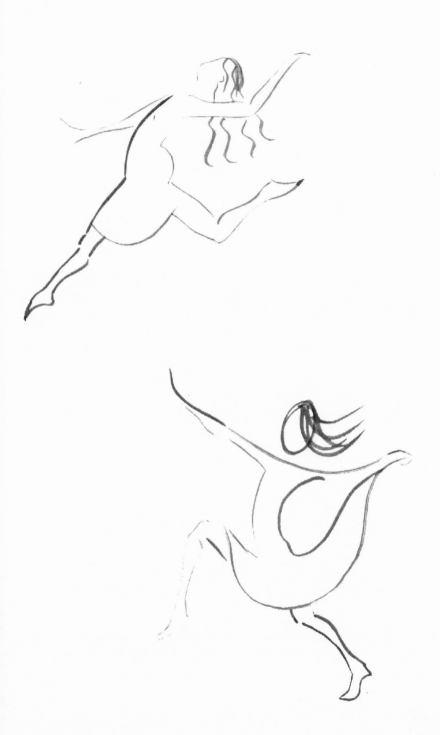

PAUSE
& REFLECT

Instructions For Making A Book

Instructions For Making A Book

Before I go, I promised you we'd make a book. This bit's incredibly fun and may be a 'new to you'. Keep an eye on my website because at some point a YouTube instruction video should appear. In the meantime...

Collect together your materials.

- Two (or more) pieces of A4 paper (or A5) for the pages.

- One piece of pretty paper or fabric for the cover, about A4 size.

- A piece of cardboard, about A4 for the cover.

- A needle and thread.

The Paper:

You'll ultimately be writing on this paper, and you can use plain white printer paper, or you could choose to look out for pretty bits of paper. You can either have double sided prettiness, or single sided prettiness, and you can always glue single-sided pretty paper back-to-back, to get double sided prettiness. The choice is entirely yours. Remember that you'll want to be able to read what you've written on these pages, so you'll need very light coloured paper and if you're choosing patterns, they have to be very pale. If you want, you can buy a card-making magazine which has lots of pretty papers in the middle (but make sure they are pale enough to write on and be read). Have fun collecting some pretty bits of paper together.

Cardboard:

For the cardboard, I used some packaging that came through the post courtesy of a big smiley delivery company. The corrugated stuff is a bit thick, but books often get delivered in thin cardboard envelopes which are ideal.

Instructions:

1. Fold an A4 page in half to make a wide rectangle (not a long narrow rectangle) and cut or tear along the crease to make 2 pieces.

2. Fold each piece in half (as if to make a greeting card). These will be your pages.

3. Repeat and make a pile of folded pages. Ultimately we will stitch them together down the crease. Your need a minimum of 16 sides to write on (one piece of A4 will make 8 sides to write on)

4. Lay one page on top of the cardboard (with the crease running vertically). Using the page as a template, draw round the page leaving an extra 1cm border on the left and right sides (but not on the top and bottom). These overhangs can be trimmed back later. Fold this cardboard neatly in half to make the cover shape.

5. Using your cardboard as a template, cut out a piece of pretty paper, or fabric to use as your cover. Leave about 1.5cm border all around your template.

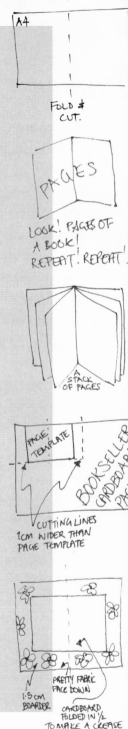

FOLD & CUT.

LOOK! PAGES OF A BOOK! REPEAT! REPEAT!

A STACK OF PAGES

PAGE TEMPLATE

BOOKSELLER CARDBOARD PACK

CUTTING LINES 1CM WIDER THAN PAGE TEMPLATE

PRETTY FABRIC FACE DOWN

1.5cm BOARDER

CARDBOARD FOLDED IN ½ TO MAKE A CREASE

6. Place the cardboard in the middle of the cover paper and tuck the paper/fabric around the cardboard to cover the edges. Using a glue stick, glue the edges of the paper/fabric to your cardboard.

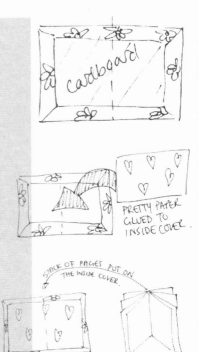

PRETTY PAPER GLUED TO INSIDE COVER.

STACK OF PAGES PUT ON THE INSIDE COVER.

7. Use one of your folded pages as a template, and cut out another piece of paper to stick to the inside of the cardboard cover, to hide the fabric or paper turnings and to hide the inside of the cardboard.

8. Assemble! Lay the opened out pages on top of the opened-out cover (so it looks like an open book).

9. Cut off a length of thread about 60cm long. Thread the needle and tie both ends of the thread together in a big knot.

10. For book binding stitches.

POKE NEEDLE IN HOLE #1

A) With the book open, make hole #1 by poking the needle into the middle of the crease and pushing down from the inside of the book, all the way through to the outside. Be careful not to pull the knot through.

B) On the front of the book, to make hole #2, push the needle into the cover crease, 2.5cm/1 inch above where the thread came out. Push it right through to the inside.

C) Now poke your needle between the two threads (NOT through the book) immediately below the knot. This makes the knot strain on the thread, not on the paper. Wiggle the thread tight.

D) On the inside of the book, make hole #3, 2.5cm/1 inch above the hole you just came out of, pushing the needle from the inside to the outside.

E) From the outside, begin travelling back down the book by poking your needle into the pre-existing hole #2, pushing your needle through to the inside.

F) From the inside, travel downwards again, make another stitch by poking your needle into pre-existing hole #3, all the way through to the outside

G) On the outside you need to make a new hole. We'll call #A, which is 2.5cm/1" below the hole you just came out of. Still travelling down you are poking your needle from the outside to the inside. You now have 3 big stitches.

H) On the inside, travel downwards and poke your needle into new hole we'll call #B.

I) On the outside, travel upwards by poking your needle back through the pre-existing hole #A.

J) On the inside, tie your thread off by tying three little knots around the nearest stitch.

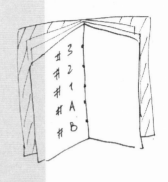

K) Poke you needle one last time, from the inside to the outside, and then carefully trim off your thread close to the hole. Hopefully the tail end is caught inside your book and it all looks nice and neat.

L) If you want, you can now trim off any excess from the pages with a craft knife, or you can leave them as is, for a more rustic look.

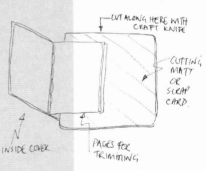

Now sit back and admire your handiwork (these little books can be quite addictive). I'd love to see your book. You can share with me by using the feedback button **www.thecompanyofsmiles.co.uk** or tagging **@thecompanyofsmiles** on instagram.

PAUSE
& REFLECT

Writing Your Life Manual

Writing Your Life Manual

Now you have this wonderful little handmade book, you can start to fill it in. What you're going to do here, is fill it with all the little tips you've written to yourself at the end of each chapter, in the Takeaways section. Remember this is a Life Manual just for you.

Write down one thing on each page which will help you keep on an even keel, or help you up when you hit a bump.

Mine has things like

"3 thankfuls a day keep my blues away"

"Low energy? Get some Sky on Your Head!"

"Need some love? Hug the World"

"Feeling glum? Grab a pencil or paintbrush and go find Indigo to dance with"

"Just want to stuff your face with cake? - have a nap. You're tired!"

To figure out what your manual needs to say, check back (review) your notes at the end of each chapter, and see what has resonated with you.

Imagine yourself one year from now. What words would you use to relay this information to that person?

Whatever words you just used, are what you write in your Life Manual.

Although if you write your notes in your most beautiful and legible handwriting, it's like sending love to your future self, its more important to just write it. Your Life Manual is better written and scruffy, than empty. (I'm sure I'm not the only one to have kept beautiful books empty because my handwriting never felt good enough)

And that's it from me for Part One. Part Two will have some more tips and techniques but until then, keep going with your thankfuls, they are a wonderful lifelong habit.

Keep sailing my friend. Chart your progress and be proud.

...and until we meet again, I wish you smooth passage and fair winds.

Mikyla
XX

PAUSE
& REFLECT

Chapter Eight
Back Matter

PAUSE
& REFLECT

Connect With Me

Connect With Me

The great thing about the technology in the world, is that it can be used to make instant connections, which even thirty years ago would have been impossible.

I do have an online presence, but a word of warning: I try to avoid spending too much time in cyberspace, preferring to be out getting some Sky On My Head and connecting with people. So I don't post as much as most.

However I'd love to hear from you and what worked (or didn't) for you. I'm busy putting together Part Two, and your feedback could really help me focus on the priorities for what I should be putting in, and what can be bumped down the road for another time. Hit the 'feedback button' at **www.thecompanyofsmiles.co.uk**. There is also the potential of a podcast because as you may have guessed, talking is like breathing for me.

Help spread the love:

If you've found this book useful, please help spread the word, to spread the love. Let's get this love planing (that's the nautical term for an exhilarating bit of surf sailing that feels like flying).

An online review would be a wonderful way to help spread the word... Amazon, Goodreads, etc

Join a face to face event:

The biggest benefit of face to face events is the opportunity to meet like minded people. I run workshops designed to bring people together, experience companionship and stimulate conversations and creativity. These workshops can be a catalyst for new connections.

www.thecompanyofsmiles.co.uk/revive-and-thrive

Keep in touch:

Sign up to the mailing list and I'll let you know when the next book comes out and where the next events and workshops are **www.thecompanyofsmiles.co.uk**

I can also be found:

Instagram: @**thecompanyofsmiles**

Facebook: /**The Company of Smiles**

...but mostly, out there getting some Sky On My Head, hugging the world.

PAUSE
& REFLECT

Thank Yous

Thank Yous

Thank you to all my beta readers - sorry you had to put up with so many typos, I'll remember to use the spellchecker next time and invest in a proof-reader if you're really lucky: Thanks especially to Rob for making me laugh (those apostrophes weren't typos - I obviously missed a key lesson at school), Yvana for her encouraging feedback and suggestions for improvement, Claire for her enthusiastic endorsement, Emma for reading my waffle and patiently navigating me around the millennial world. To Sara for putting some commas back in.

To Hannah Carter-Brown for being so much fun to work with on layouts, to Anne at ScrivenVirgin for taming my typing, to Sam Boyce for the first assessment, to Lynette Cresswell for making me believe in myself as a writer.

To Charlie Macksey for inspiring me to get inky, to Quentin Blake for his great lessons, to Eddie Reader and Mike Rosenberg for singing so nicely to me as I type.

To Mary for her never ending belief in me and for having the original idea to make a book which is beautiful. To David for his inspiring love and his skin. To my children for emptying the dishwasher and their copious supply of hugs. To my daughter for pre-selling this book to anyone who would listen (and probably a few who tried not to). To Karen for being my haven and picking me up when I fell and for picking me up when I fell and for (you get the idea).

And finally to Mrs Stoner's Group, and to Auntie Jan, for always loving me. You have no idea how much I love you all (although you may do now).

Team

Design Layout **hcbDesigns.co.uk**

Cover Design **nathanburtondesign.com**

Publisher **thecompanyofsmiles.co.uk**

References and Further Reading

Page 27   www.yellowstonepark.com "Wolf Reintroduction Changes Ecosystem in Yellowstone" by Brodie Farquhar. June 2020

Page 48   www.ted.com 'Why Ambitious Women Have Flat Heads'

Page 78   Esther Gokhale "8 Steps to a Pain-Free Back"

Page 86   NHS 'Couch to 5k' app

Page 107   www.SAD.uk SADAssociation, PO Box 989, Steyning BN44 3HG

Page 108   Michael Mosley "Trust Me I'm A Doctor/ Should I worry about Seasonal Affective Disorder?"

Page 113   www.asthma.org.uk. See also 'volatile organic compounds' and 'cleaning products' on this site

Page 135   Dr David Hamilton "Little Book of Kindness"

Page 142   Jim Rohn "You are the average of the five people you spend the most time with."

Page 146   Mel Robbins "When your problems are enormous it's the littlest things that get you moving"

Page 168   "The Creative Brain" by Dr David Eagleman
www.creativebrainmovie.com

Page 184   Youtube 'Yoga with Adriene'

Page 196   Alain De Botton alaindebotton.com

Page 198   www.truity.com/test/type-finder-personality-
test-new

Page 206   The Pursuit of Happyness, Dir. Gabriele
Muccino 2006

Page 220   BBC Radio 4 'In Business'

Page 221   Alex Soojung-Kim Pang

Page 227   www.yorspace.org

Page 227   www.co-housing.org.uk

Page 230   "The Biggest Little Farm" Dir John Chester
2018

Page 233   Tiny steps inspired by Julia Cameron "The
Artist's Way"